Enneagram
Dialogs on Prayer

Enneagram Dialogs on Prayer

Rosaleen O'Sullivan, R.S.M.

BIBAL Press
N. Richland Hills, Texas

BIBAL Press
An imprint of D. & F. Scott Publishing, Inc.
P.O. Box 821653
N. Richland Hills, TX 76182
1–888–788–2280
bibal@cmpu.net
www.cmpu.net/public/bibal

Printed in the United States of America

02 01 00 99 98   5 4 3 2 1

Library of Congress Cataloging-in-Publication Data
O'Sullivan, Rosaleen, 1928-
   Enneagram dialogs on prayer / Rosaleen O'Sullivan.
   p. cm.
Includes bibliographical references.

ISBN 0-94-103771-1
1. Prayer--Catholic Church. 2. Enneagram. I. Title.
BV215 .O78 1998
248.3'2--dc21
                                        98-40249
                                        CIP

In Gratitude

To the staff of the Institute for Spiritual Leadership in Chicago, especially Suzanne Zuercher, O.S.B., and Paul Robb, S.J., who introduced us to the enneagram in a practical, day-to-day way, and, six years later, led us through advanced studies. Thanks also to my fellow journeyers at ISL and all we learned from each other. They are still the living paradigm for me of the enneagram.

To my community, the Sisters of Mercy, Burlingame Regional Community, who requested and responded so eagerly to enneagram studies, and who encouraged me constantly. My special appreciation to all who shared so honestly on videotape, that workshop participants could learn from their lived experience.

And, in a special way, to those who shared from their own prayer life histories, one-on-one with me.

To Claudio Naranjo, whom I have not met personally, but whose essay On the Psychology of Meditation *clarified for me, on a spiritual world scale, much of what I was hearing, and gave me the framework for listening and writing.*

All these and many, many unnamed share in the truth and any valued content in this book. My share has been to listen carefully and to articulate, hopefully, some measure of that truth.

Contents

Acknowledgments

So many people over so many years have contributed to the making and content of this book, and most of them may not realize that their words, comments, and insights about their own experiences in the matter of prayer have helped form these pages. Nor could I name them, though I did enjoy facilitating their groups, and am glad to have this chance to offer them my thanks.

The full manuscript was capably critiqued by Barbara Moran, R.S.M. and Celeste Rouleau, R.S.M., who, along with their fine suggestions, corrections, and insights, were a real source of encouragement.

The parts of the manuscript about their own enneagram energies were read by members of my community, who gave me feedback and more insights. I am grateful to these Sisters of Mercy for their time, their generous help, and their honesty about their own experiences: Patricia Beirne, Julia Howard, Suzanne Krawczyk, Barbara Moran, Yvette Perrault, Carmen Rodriguez, Marie Eloise Rosenblatt, Celeste Rouleau, Patricia Williams.

Thanks, also, to Don Bisson, F.M.S., Tom Hand, S.J., and Gene O'Sullivan for their valuable input on the #234 prayer, the chakras, and the #567 prayer respectively.

The following will recognize themselves from videotaped dialogs which included some significant comments on prayer included in this text: Beverly Dunn, S.P., Charleen Koenig, R.S.M., Marietta McGannon, R.S.M., Joan Marie O'Donnell, R.S.M., Janet Rozzano, R.S.M., and Susan Vickers, R.S.M.

Thanks to my very thorough proofreader, Ellen FitzGerald, R.S.M., and to my guide through computer labyrinths and styles, Carolyn Marie Krohn, R.S.M. And a big sigh of grateful relief for Julia Howard, into whose capable hands and enthusiastic energy all the demands of publishing were left. What would I do without my community?

ACKNOWLEDGMENTS

Beyond these there is the sizable blend of group dialogs on tape or in written responses from workshop participants, and all of these lent words or tone or depth or echo to these pages, if not their names, and have taught me very much indeed. Thank you all, named and unnamed!

Introduction

The genesis of this book lies in simple conversations, in the spontaneous sharings of small groups of workshop participants, and in the honest reflections of some people on their own prayer journeys. This book, then, is a collected reflection from dialogs I have had over some fifteen years, and in which you are invited to participate. To a respectful listening-in, I have added the shape of my own enneagram training at the Institute for Spiritual Leadership in Chicago, and the further knowledge gained through leading over a thousand participants through basic enneagram studies.

It was some of these participants who gave me the idea of putting the workshop experience into writing in book form. They simply asked me why I did not do so, claiming that they would gladly revisit the experience in their own leisure time, and would appreciate the chance to mull over points which fed, inspired, supported, or moved them on. It is primarily for these people that this book is written, with hopes that others may find in it some encouragement and light, not only for themselves on their spiritual journey, but for any with whom and for whom they may minister. I am thinking here of spiritual directors in particular, and how the material in these dialogs may offer added understanding of how the different triads consider God and prayer, as well as their individual preferences in method and ideals.

So this book is for the spiritual pilgrim, the pray-er, who wants to grow in the inner awarenesses of simple and naturally contemplative modes of prayer, reflection, or just holy being. It presupposes knowledge and some lived experience of the enneagram, some steps along its conversion journey, the honest and often humbling acceptance of previously unrecognized personal blind spots and faults, and a willingness to look again at blocks and gifts. It is these foundations on which understandings of prayer in the enneagram rest.

For basic enneagram work or introductory material, please consult the many books available, some of which are listed among the reference materials at the end of this book.

Invitation to Dialog

C onsider this book an invitation extended to you personally. You have already found a source of enlightenment and practical self-knowledge in the wisdom of the enneagram, in how it holds up to you the reflection of the gifts and strengths you have to offer; of your unattended prides, fixations, and what you defend or avoid; along with a very useful beneath-the-skin understanding of others. This book is an invitation to go deeper, deeper in yourself than personality flaws or admirable talents, to a realm the enneagram calls the zone of essence, or truth, or soul. This is an invitation to spend time with soul, and its nourishment, prayer.

If you have really entered the journey of conversion the enneagram presents to us, you have found you are not really who you thought you were. The "I am good because I am . . ." is a pride, a mask, albeit a comforting one from childhood, that falsely identifies a person; and indeed, because it is a mask, a persona, it belies the one who wears it. The ego is the force behind this character fixation, this lie, and the enneagram helps us to see through it, to see into the realm of truth. It is here, this realm of truth or essence or soul, that we leave the false truths of ego to find our true Self. This is where "home" is, our rich and priceless realm of genuine being and true intuition. Prayer seems one good way to reach this realm of true self.

But a word about how the enneagram introduces us to it. If you imagine three concentric circles inside each other: the center circle is this zone of essence, the outer one is the zone of external reality, and between them lies the middle zone of fantasy or ego. As Jerome Wagner says in his 1980 paper, "The Enneagram System of Personality Typology":

> The person who lives in the middle zone is not in contact with the environment but with his side of the inner zone, which he presents to the environment as a mask. On the other hand, the environment is not in contact with the authentic self, but with the outside of the middle zone or mask, which the individual presents to it. This middle zone shields, protects, and subdues the authentic self, and the person expends his energy in maintaining and developing the mask. (Wagner 1980, 14)

It is in this middle zone that the ego keeps us in fixations, avoidances, defenses, and all the false armor of which the enneagram gives warning, keeping the zone of self and the zone of external reality apart, and out of touch. So, if you would move into the inner realms of prayer, you would want to approach them with honesty, because they lie beneath that middle zone. It takes humility to cross that zone while keeping in touch with external reality. Your enneagram type has its own crossing journey and its own mode of being in silent, inner prayer. In fact, it has its own mode of reaching there in a simple, natural way. This is, in brief, the subject of this book.

Inner Prayer

You may genuinely wonder at the term "inner prayer" since prayer, by its nature, would always have an "inner." But think of what you consider prayer. Is it interceding for one who needs God's help, praising God, pleading for personal needs, psalmody, holding a conversation with God, songs and hymns that move the heart? Or is it one of many other forms, such as the rosary, pondering Scripture, saying favorite vocal prayers, attending liturgy, or a formal system of meditation? We have many ways of being in prayer and of expressing it as our own.

Most of you have recognized a level deeper than these expressions, a sort of spring that wells and draws without words, an impetus that can lead to expression, but often is enough in itself. It is sort of a natural leaning, a preference

that you take for granted, and it is there when you want to be
alone, just you and God, without an agenda. You might find
some of these words descriptive:

being quietly in my mind

without words

my heart prays

I have a sense of belonging to God

my whole being is centered in God

just being in God.

The enneagram suggests that our natural head or heart or gut
energy leans us spontaneously into a certain "at home" inner
level of prayer, a certain inner impetus with which we are at
ease. When this is brought to consciousness, it is a source of
simple grace and gratitude—an acceptance of a quiet gift
familiar since childhood, but not articulated. The hope of this
book is that articulation.

You will be reading in this book quite a few words about
these basically wordless inner prayer energies, along with the
head, heart, and gut prayer forms they lead to. Though I may
use as examples famous pray-ers, saints, and mystics as encouragement in the journey, what I discuss is not their state of
prayer, but that inner impetus that they honored as a beginning. This book offers only the very basic modes of prayer
energy that seem to be natural to the different enneatypes, a
starting place, somewhere comfortable to be on one's prayer
journey, a gift of one's own to appreciate. It will look at modes
or forms of prayer that could be called contemplative, but not
at the contemplative state in which the great pray-ers lived, a
state reached by a long, disciplined, and transforming journey. The basic model considered is Christian contemplative
prayer, but the energies are, of course, the universal ones of
the enneagram and are, hopefully, universally helpful.

Some Enneagram Basics

Assuming you have already studied the enneagram and are familiar with your own type, I will offer only a partial review of some main elements.

Given the spiritual subject matter approached here, it would seem good to start with an enneagram-friendly view of God. In "The Enneagram System of Personality Typology," Jerome Wagner begins his "core statements" with the nine faces of God, from the anthropology/theology of Sufism:

> This theology states that each person is born with certain gifts or qualities that reflect the divine image. Each individual reflects some facet of the divine face. It is both one's privilege and destiny to be stamped with this divine seal. These gifts or strengths are one's contribution to the human community. (8)

> Just as any good can be misused or misappropriated, so can a person misappropriate his gift. Instead of using it for the common good of others, he uses it for himself. The individual takes "pride" in his gift. Instead of contributing to the common good, he uses it for his own good. He attempts to preserve himself by his gifts, to make himself good, lovable, secure. The gift becomes armor to protect oneself rather than balm for the common weal. (9)

Thus, God's reflection and gift becomes a negative caricature, a good that I overuse and distort, but still pride myself on, not able to see that what I hold as a "good" in me is really a false pride. This pride is defended from early in life, becomes encrusted with self-preserving ideas and strong feelings and passions, and grows into what the enneagram holds as one of the "nine manifestations of a disordered heart." (11) ". . . It is this corruption which is sin . . . Sin is like being bent . . . When an object is bent, it will be misshapen, or will malfunction, or will fail to function at all. A bent arrow or a bent gun will miss the mark." (11) Using Wagner's points, we can chart the ideas in this way:

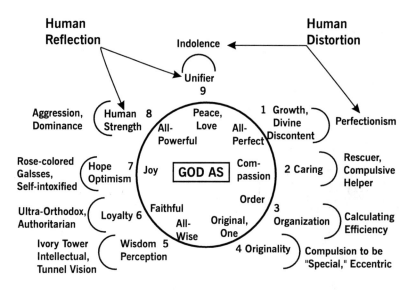

The enneagram invites us back to our gift, and to balance. But the way through the zone of ego is a long one, through fixated and idealized patterns, passions, defenses, avoidances, and traps, along with a host of insights through which the enneagram helps us call up from the unconscious what hinders us in a healthy journey to our essence.

Fixations

"Enneagram" comes from two Greek words, *ennea* (nine) and *grammos* (points), referring to the nine points around a circle, which we have seen as the nine faces of God. Each reflection of God is a type at its best—its giftedness. But each reflection is also a facet of the whole human person, as reflected in the circle of wholeness suggested by the enneagram diagram. This could symbolize the wholeness of the individual or of all humankind. However, we do not hold these facets equally until we come to a mature integration of our whole person. Early in life, we lean heavily toward one, and as it takes over our self-image and as we defend it as a personal good, we move into compulsive patterns and reach a fixation. The enneagram has names for these fixations into which the ego is unconsciously bound, names that label the patterns which are, at root, reactions to a falsely assumed lack of the gift:

#1 ego-resent

#2 ego-flatterer

#3 ego-go or -vanity

#4 ego-melancholy

#5 ego-stinge

#6 ego-coward

#7 ego-plan

#8 ego-venge

#9 ego-indolent.

These fixations are so constant in us that we are unaware how much we are caught in them, and it takes some honesty to see and accept what the enneagram tells us of ourselves. With recognition comes the challenge to put on my fixation and be or do or feel the energy. With active acceptance comes a bit of humility and conscious healing.

Avoiding and Defending

A variety of things and events can threaten my pride, but I tend to avoid one particular threat to my view of my self, the one thing that I fear could prove it false. The "perfect" #1 avoids anger as not right, imperfect; the "helpful" #2 avoids personal needs as irrelevant in the face of others' needs; the "born administrator" #3 avoids failure as a collapse of a carefully crafted image of success; the "different" #4 avoids anything ordinary, wasting energy in redoing things with a unique personal twist; the "wise" #5 avoids lack, especially the emptiness of not knowing enough to really produce; the "loyal" #6 avoids disobedience as a threat to security; the "just fine" #7 avoids pain and any other negative; the "can do anything" strength of the #8 avoids weakness, and considers tenderness weak; the "peaceful" #9 avoids conflict as unsettling, even trying to keep it out of consciousness.

Each type has its own technique to ensure that the avoidance works: #1 reacts to correct what is not "right," thinking that it deflects anger at imperfection, but it does not; #2 represses personal needs, not even owning them; #3 identifies with any role that will ensure success; #4 uses artistic sublimation to invest experiences as special; #5 withdraws into isolation to collect data for more knowledge; #6 projects blame on anyone considered deviant; #7 sublimates any negatives and plans them away; #8 simply denies what might be a challenge; #9 counters conflict with something brain-deadening, like sleep or nonthinking monotonous activity.

In this way, we keep ourselves well-armored, not conscious of the layers of plate we have built up. These prides, fixes, avoidances, and defenses will be spelled out in practical descriptions in the book, especially in the "Let Me Say Hello" sections that precede each of the three energy centers. These centers: head, heart, and gut are the distinct energies that carry the main differences in prayer and will be addressed at length descriptively. Also addressed, but more obliquely, will be the passions and virtues, and the triads of wings and arrows.

The Passions and Virtues

Each of the types is associated with a negative emotion that seems to "set the emotional tone of his personality." (35) It is so pervasive, so constant, that, if we think of it at all, we consider it part of who we are, part of our personality pattern. These negative emotions are called passions, and are the basic human faults historically referred to as the capital sins that undermine human good. With a little reflection, you will see how each is a fit for the enneatype's fixation. "Put simply, they are a false assumption (idealized self-image) plus energy." (35) Just a simple list of them here will suffice, since they must come into the text as definite hindrances to prayer: #1 anger, #2 pride, #3 deceit, #4 envy, #5 avarice, #6 fear, #7 gluttony, #8 lust, #9 indolence. As you see, deceit and fear have been added to the basic seven capital vices. The particular strengths which the enneagram calls virtues are not just opposites to the passions, but helps to wholeness for each type: #1 serenity, as the person accepts lack of perfection, and settles for gradual, not immediate, growth; #2 humility, as the person acknowledges personal limits and needs; #3 honesty, for the person who has hidden defects under a fail-proof image of success; #4 equanimity, a soul-balance as the person accepts with contentment the reality of the here-and-now; #5 detachment, as the person shares inner goods and knowledge, not clinging to a false privacy; #6 courage to accept inner authority and to face new things; #7 sobriety, setting limits on options and enjoyments, balancing negatives with the idealistic; #8 compassion and sensitivity for those less strong; #9 diligence in work and skills and in becoming more conscious of life. These aids to self-knowledge and conversion are strong gifts that the enneagram offers to those who will work for a mature personal integration. Passions must be faced and virtues pursued if a realistic sense of the enneagram's invitation is to bear fruit.

Wings and Arrows

If you wonder at the variety in each enneatype, you will find a discussion of the wings of each type and the arrows in the diagram helpful. This will, however, not be that discussion, but just a mention of them.

The wings are the types that flank each number, and lend their own distinct energy to it, at least in some degree. A strong wing lends the look of that wing, sometimes so strongly that it takes over, and aspects of the persona (the mask or "look" of personality that you present to others, and by which others recognize you) are shifted clearly to that side. Too much persona in a wing might be an imbalance, might dominate your own type enough to muddy up your clarity of purpose. The wings of your type carry their own distinct positives and negatives, strengths that you can call on and traps to be aware of. As you study your wings, you will find a supply of shadow material, gifts and faults that you were not in touch with, that were not acknowledged. In other words, you possess a broader spectrum of traits and talents than your own enneagram type description offers. You have more basic riches to share.

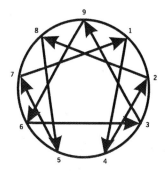

The three types that are your basic energies of being are augmented chiefly by two movements of becoming. These are called the arrows—the lines in the enneagram diagram that connect to your own number.

These arrows always follow the same distinct pattern around the enneagram, a map of movement around the whole. You will notice that one arrow points toward and one away from your number. The one pointing toward your own number brings, the enneagram suggests, the strong aspects of that other type for you to use; or, more correctly, when you find yourself functioning well, look for traits of the type at the other end of the arrow that you are using positively. Likewise, when you are in some dysfunction, you will probably be able to read about it in descriptions of the type to which the arrow of your own number points. But this does not mean you cultivate one type and avoid the other, because you are really offered the pluses and minuses of both types to actively enrich your own. For example, after you have experienced the downers of going with the arrow, and have worked through them, you will surprise yourself with new gifts to use from that source. These theories of wings and arrows are not always presented to seminar participants, but they do help you to see how dynamic and moving the whole enneagram reality is.

The dynamic qualities of the enneagram have been especially helpful to me in my ministry of spiritual direction, not only the practical negatives of fixation, avoidance, defense, and any other compulsive trap of the seeker, but the gifts, the virtues, the positive strengths, and God's invitations to grow and integrate. As a #4, I find that I unconsciously look for the beauty in the person—beneath the weeds or brambles perhaps—but as a promise of bloom while the hard work of gardening goes on through the seasons.

So much for the review, which is, admittedly, a bit sparse, and on to the purpose of the book—prayer and the enneagram. The next chapter gives the setting of a workshop, facilitated many times, which is the basis for all the materials following.

2

The Dialog Begins

Y ou may have had the experience of seeing someone wake up to a gift that has always been there within, but is fully recognized and owned for the first time. It has been my privilege to see this each time I have led groups in an enneagram workshop on prayer. It is freeing for people to learn that they can be simply at prayer without having to follow a strict formula, a schema of some sort, or the expectations of others, but to let themselves be drawn by God's Spirit and their own. It is for them a relief and a welcome light to hear others' very different modes of being with God, especially in the same shared time, place, and experience. Let me replay the scene for you briefly. After I have led the group in relaxation exercises, inviting them to let go of tensions and their busy lives, I guide them in a very simple form of centering prayer, and leave them in silence. The profound stillness and sense of the holy is something I and others who lead such groups have come to expect, though it always impresses me anew. After some time, I invite them to a gentle closure, to reflect on their experience, and to journal if they wish. The sense of quiet remains. Then I suggest that they silently respond, as they are able, to questions that I propose about their experience, such as symbols, images, movement, idea/thought content, the leader's words, or difficulties. These responses are then shared in small groups composed of people with the same enneagram number, and here some of the delight and surprise occurs as so many find kindred experiences, present and past. Openness follows, and often a kind of relief at not being alone, at being easily understood and understanding. But the surprises are not over. Discussion in the full group affords more.

Enneatypes 891

Usually I first invite responses from the 891 groups because what they say will be simple and direct, though will sound a bit unfinished to some others, a bit empty perhaps. Here are some of the typical responses from these pray-ers:

> *I don't know what the leader said. I dropped out early on and was just "there."*
>
> *Too many words.*
>
> *What's a "movement"? I couldn't respond to that question.*
>
> *It was all just being with God.*
>
> *There was God and there was me.*
>
> *It went too fast.*
>
> *Nothing happened, no images, no ideas or such, but a real peace.*
>
> *I had an image—no, I guess it was a symbol for me, a great white light.*
>
> *Come to think of it, I left the leader soon after we started and there was nothing, a kind of darkness, I guess, but I did not want to leave at the end.*

Other people in the general group listen and start to realize how different from their own experience this commentary is. They begin to see that enneatypes 891 tend to negate prayer content such as words, ideas or thoughts, movement or feelings, and that even images and symbols are few.

Enneatypes 234

The 234 center usually offers a striking contrast to the first group, and can sound almost flamboyant in contrast. A #3 or #4 may start, with a comment that does not get inside the experience, such as: "It was nice." "How quiet it was. I like that." Then, often enough, a #2 will open the feeling level of this group with something like: "My heart seemed to expand. I could feel all this warmth and peace flowing out into my whole body, and I felt God loving me." To which, perhaps, a #8 will say, "Is she for real? Pure exaggeration!" If this happens, the responses shut down, become cautious, and the 234 group becomes less spontaneous as they nurture their image ego, easily bruised. If it does not happen, or if the leader can salvage the good name of the 234, the sharing continues more on target with such comments as:

Yes, I felt myself loving God. (And here a #2 will often gesture toward the area of the heart.)

I seemed to move deeper into myself, and kept going—it felt like down—until I settled into God deep down within me.

There were colors in my inner movement, just areas of color I passed through, beautiful colors that made me feel good and close to God.

I sensed a warm, peaceful, loving presence.

When I reached a center point I seemed to open to God, like a flower opens. That was the image I rested with in God.

These people do not speak easily of their inner experience. But when they do, the expressions are of image, color, movement, and feelings.

Enneatypes 567

This center does not seem to have as many words around inner experiences, though it is easier to follow what this triad says. There is not too much of the #891's easygoing thereness, or the #234 group's feelings, movements, and images, but there is usually clarity:

The leader's words were a big help to keep me focused.

I like the quiet directions, the spaces, and then the silence, which really invited God's presence.

As long as the quiet words continued I was prayerful and quiet, but in the pauses I found it hard not to allow irrelevant thoughts.

It was a very peaceful experience.

I found myself inviting Jesus to be with me in my center.

Jesus was with me as soon as I closed my eyes.

When I responded to the words to move inward I was caught by "where is inward?" for awhile. Then, with some effort, I shook loose of that and just listened and tried to go with the words.

It took me until the end to become quiet and still and in God's presence.

#567 people acknowledge that words are basically important to them, with much of the prayer content in ideas and thoughts, to which images can be added. Feelings and inner movements seem usually unattended or even absent, though images can carry real power. Images of Jesus seem to occur more frequently in this group.

This brief tap into the experiences that open our workshop day on the enneagram and prayer may give you some idea of the different tones of responses to the same simple prayer. There are, of course, many more, but the same triad expresses the same cluster of responses no matter where or when or among whom the day is given. At this point, these three groups of dialog quotes will serve as a bird's eye view of what I hope to expand in the chapters immediately following. It seems, though, a clearer perspective to reverse the order and discuss the 567 enneatypes first, then the 234, with the 891 rounding off the enneagram prayer preferences. Perhaps a word would not be amiss here about the fact that as people grow in prayer, they seem to broaden their preferences and to depend less on the fundamental ones. More exposure to this movement would be needed, but from my dialogs with steady pray-ers and my experience as a spiritual director I have become aware that people may grow into an ease with other prayer forms, especially those of the enneatype "going against the arrow," or those of a wing in another triad. As you read on, I suggest you keep in mind two qualifying features of this material:

1. Most of the people involved in these sessions had made, or desired to make, a definite place for prayer in

their lives, and many had experienced years of prayer in religious communities.

2. Regardless of the length of experience involved, what surfaces (and what these pages dwell on) is the basic orientation—the connatural movements if you will—of personal prayer in the enneagram types and triads. We are not dealing here with higher or infused states of prayer or contemplation, but rather with the natural receptivities on which and out of which the Holy Spirit builds.

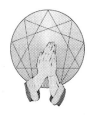

3

#567—Let Me Say Hello

Although this is not a book on the basics of the enneagram, it seems appropriate to include an introduction to each of the types, drawn from the comments of people who have lived with the enneagram for a while. Each triad will begin in this way—with a composite comment portrait of each enneatype in its own words. These words can be disturbingly honest to those who have not yet worked with the hard insights gained from the enneagram, especially those regarding our hidden compulsions and flaws.

Here the types personally introduce themselves in dialog.

Enneatype 5

You would probably have to be the one to say hello to me first. I tend to stand back and observe people before I invest myself. In fact, I feel sort of invisible or insignificant as far as presenting myself personally goes, but as far as what I *know*—well, that's another matter. All my life I've known myself to be intellectually probing, or that I know things others don't, or maybe can't know. When events or people don't measure up to my inner observation tower I easily tag them as "stupid." It's a word I use a lot, at least inside. I'm not at my most comfortable with people, because they are unpredictable on a feeling level and they can invade my space. You see, I try to keep things objective and not fuzzed up by feelings. I keep things in control through my head, through logic, through thought processes, and to do that effectively I need my privacy, my

17

own uninvaded space. I am kind of a natural monk who can sit alone for hours to think, observe, and compute, with little need to talk or relate. Sharing is hard for me. People say I am stingy with my responses, my feelings, my knowledge; but inside myself, I sense more of an emptiness than a stinginess.

After I've learned all I can, there still seems to be an empty hole that sets me to take in, to gather, collect, even horde, and at the same time to be afraid that the emptiness can never be filled, no matter how much I know, or prepare, or read. I guess I am more of a taker than a giver or one who produces. Yet, I can be very detached from what I collect, I can live very frugally. In fact, I pride myself on how little I need or use, though people tell me that's just another stingy aspect of my temperament. I cringe at that word, "stingy." I'm trying to work at giving more of myself, at getting involved concretely and not just through the constructs in my head, which I see now are quite pervasive. It's too hard to just *do* something without thinking it all through first, too hard to keep control of, say, errors and their consequences. I feel so safe behind my eyes, where I can look out, observe all things, take in all I want, and no one else can see inside me. That's why emotional involvement would be so hard for me, not only because it is fuzzy and messy, but because someone else might see inside me. Maybe I've always protected myself from physical or emotional involvement, but if I work at it, I can tend to my feelings, and even have strong ones. I just don't have words for them when that happens. In fact, I'm surprised that I found all the words I just did—and about myself! It may take a lot of self-acceptance, besides knowledge, and a willingness to *do* and not just think (often I spend so much time in my head on a project that I take it for granted it is done), but I really can become an involved, productive, and original contributor to society.

Enneatype 6

You know, I'm really kind of likable, and can even be warm and engaging, but you may find me just a smidge cautious as I greet you. People can really draw out my loyalties, especially

my family and friends, and I'll stick by them, be very dependable. Dependable is my middle name—dependable and responsible. Friends tell me I am often over-responsible.
Somehow, I get caught into what is expected of me, but I do
feel better when I know all is as it should be. I like things pre-
dictable, like a clear right and wrong. I'm coming to realize
that all these rights and wrongs, or expectations, or rules, or
structures are outside of me, and do not really substitute for
well-informed and clear decisions in conscience, but it is very
hard indeed for me to come to my own decisions through my
own inner authority. That process is something I find hard to
trust, though I know I've got to learn it. I get trapped into the
security of having others "know" for me. For a long time, I
considered disobedience a grave sin and could not understand those who would choose their obedience, or disagree
with authority. If I didn't have an authority for direction there
was ambiguity—and I have enough doubts as it is. Lately I've
found it harder to point accusing fingers, to blame others for
things like civil disobedience, or for defending personal con-
victions in the face of authority. I call myself cautious or pru-
dent or loyal to the system, but I know these are just labels for
my constant companion, fearfulness. Yet, I hate to be called a
coward. Every so often, I find myself rather courageous, genuinely facing my own inner fear, and then taking on a danger
or a challenge. And when I do, I recognize a feeling of being
disgusted, fed up, with my constant fear, and taking it in
hand, sometimes without even thinking. Thinking is an unre-
lenting tactic of mine, which I hardly know I do all the time. I
suspect there is often a better guide than thinking, than
depending on the reasonable, the logical, the law. I suspect
that a trust in my own inner authority will lead perhaps to the
freedom to stand on my own, and to know from a deeper,
truer source within me. It will take time and courage and risk,
it will take more honest naming of my fear, especially the fear
of trusting and using my own authority. Even then, I am cautious of the catch involved, the catch of taking over, of supply-
ing the authority myself, of becoming authoritarian,
especially over those who are mutually loyal. You see? I do

struggle between doubt and fear, but as I see these things, I know I am coming to balance.

Enneatype 7

Hi there! Isn't this enneagram neat? I just love being a #7. Wouldn't want to be anything else. This whole system of nine points and how it all interrelates just fascinates me. In fact, just about any system fascinates me, how it all goes together. I even like making up new systems to make things work out more positively. Positive. You could say I'm a very positive person. I've often been called an optimist because I see the bright side. Any other side I avoid. Can't stand pain. Don't like to accept negative or dark stuff. People should be happy. I'm happy! It gets me when people are down. Smile! Let the sun shine in. I smile a lot and I try to make people feel joyful, never gloomy. We need more parties, more rainbows. People tell me I smile most of the time. Must be because I am such a happy person. My motto? Life is fun. I easily enjoy myself, and I enjoy people, food, doing things, and all kinds of experiences. Keeps me young. I'm a Peter Pan at heart, a *puer aeternus*, always young. Guess that's why I have such a young-looking face, as I'm often told. I have lots of energy. I really enjoy activity, getting involved, having lots of options. One thing I often do on a given day is keep all my options open, choose the ones that are the most fun, and do as many as I can. Responsibility? Superficiality? Well, I can be responsible; it's just not something I usually dwell on. But I don't like to be called superficial. After all, I really do invest myself and my many energies, though I'm not a real stick-to-it person. I'm good at planning. My mind is always buzzing with plans, and I even replan before I get started carrying one out. The fun is in the planning, not so much in the work or the doing that follows. I've noticed lately that I plan away pain or any negative reality. Maybe I keep going from option to option, or plan to plan just to avoid the dark side of things. Maybe, too, that's why I'm always "up," why I tend to sublimate, see only the bright side. That must be why the idea of moderation is so hard, why "temperance" sounds so nasty. It all seems so dull.

But no, I'll try. I know that the idea of more of any good thing is my hook. Before I know it, there is the threat of gluttony. I've got to aim at being grounded, being more middle-of-the-road, and getting in and seeing through to the end more of what I can so easily plan, even when it's boring or tiresome or a challenge to just see it through. Who knows? I may become mild as well as pleasant; I may not only sparkle but become solidly creative.

4

#567 Prayer: Some Basics

If you find yourself in this triad, you may not be aware of how strongly and frequently your intellectual filter functions, or how insufficiently you might trust other modes of knowing, such as intuition, feeling, or bodily, instinctive knowing. You depend on your outer senses, especially your eyes, to observe, assess, and collect knowledge. Because you have an immediate perception response to what you draw in, you may sense that you have a large and active inner world, one that often enough is filled and interesting. In prayer there is a real trap, then, in gathering more data, in letting your prayer be wholly taken up with thinking, comparing, judging, instead of opening to quiet or to affective movements. One very profitable movement, which you may already do well, is to "see" Jesus, to allow him to be your companion, guide, and model, and in time, intimate friend and healer.

Wisdom

Do you find the search for wisdom quite attractive? Whether with Jesus as wisdom figure or with broader symbols and meanings, you may follow the invitation to ponder, to understand with your very being, to become wisdom itself, and even, in this way, to become one with all existence. Your enneatypes can feel drawn into contemplation of the universe and from it feel integrated within, and to sense and be impelled by your own place in the cosmos. Lights in prayer are important for you, and give you direction and strength, assuring you of the value of your prayer. You may doubt that value at times when there is a lack of (intellectual) light, or a fear of some darkness, of not being able to "see," but perhaps the experience is an invitation to move beyond intellectual perception to the judgment of the heart which is wisdom. In this darkness you may find assurance in, perhaps, a sense of Presence.

Scripture

This is, of course, a mine of riches for you, even more so than for other enneatypes. Because you rely much on your eyes and mind, The Book becomes constant and easy nourishment for you as you plumb the depths of the words, pondering the scenes and events, exploring the meanings, whether they be clear or obscure. Words are a ready vehicle of prayer for you. Yours is a natural aptitude for prayer forms that flow from Scripture, such as liturgy, chants, and petitioning prayer—so much so that #6s seem to be among the best liturgists, with their care for truth, for the Word, for preaching (hopefully within time limits), and for the steadying ritual requirements of a group. All this can flow quite profitably from your prayer and meditation. Not only can 567s use your senses effectively and encourage quiet ponderings on what you have taken in, but you like to see how to do something with your prayer afterwards. This is why liturgical groups, among others, benefit from your participation. In your own inner prayer, you probably find comfort in seeing into the persons and scenes of Scripture, and engaging them in dialog. This use of words and seeing is natural to you.

Icons

The same at-homeness that the words of Scripture and liturgy invite comes also from other uses of the senses and the mind. Visual images such as pictures, statues, crucifixes, candles, and Scripture scenes in any form draw out the prayer energy of the 567. Music, with or without words, also does so, especially the quieting, repetitive influence of chant. Perhaps one of your most favorite forms of prayer, icon gazing, can help you, as well as others who pray from other energies, to understand the flow pattern involved. Let us say you have a favorite icon, an icon of Jesus, as many 567s prefer, and you settle yourself to quietness and to simply gazing at the face or form before you. You find yourself gazing, concentrating, and then being absorbed by all that the picture means to you. Jesus becomes somehow present, becomes the reality as the one-dimensional icon fades, and you find yourself in union with Jesus, absorbed by his presence, as you are drawn into his person. Your prayer has carried you out of yourself (your head and its senses) and beyond the symbol into union with what the icon represents. When such union happens, the icon can be relinquished, its energy cherished. It is, of course, the intriguing form of icon art that facilitates all this. The flat, non-dimensional perspective gives the feel of easy passage through the figure, as if it is merely a veil—albeit a solid one. It has done its work of luring you out of your head, your busy thoughts, your over-full mind, into the uncluttered realm of the simple Other. As we shall see later, this freeing shift is healing for the 567 pray-er, and can happen with any meaningful outer form.

Contemplation

This, for the #567 is the often-expressed traditional mode of "gazing at" God with the whole being, usually led there by the eyes and the inner sense. God can lure you in any way, of course, but your usual relation with God is through Jesus. Jesus himself is the icon of God, "the image of the invisible God" (Col 1:15), in whom "the fullness of deity resides in bodily form" (Col 2:9), a reliable other to draw you and your energies outward, and into a peace and union. As we shall discuss later, this prayer form is outer-directed.

What Helps

Some suggestions follow immediately on what we just discussed.

Even if the absorbing prayer above does not occur, it is helpful to receive an image and let it evoke a response. Notice the words "receive" and "evoke," in other words, a more receptive mode than your usual one of collecting ideas and pursuing them to keep your mind comfortably busy. A little trust in non-intellectual energies, hard as it is to sustain, goes a long way here. It is growthful.

Another relevant aid is to cooperate with your attraction to imitate Jesus and his qualities. Get absorbed in them, embody them. Embodiment is always the challenge: to connect your mind to your body; to live out in actuality what your mind only pictures or peruses; to become more whole by cooperating in a meaningful lived response to God. Anything that moves you prayerfully from your idea level into actual experience is a blessing for you.

You may have a mighty aversion to it, but body movement such as simple gestures, dance, and yoga help keep you connected to the physical, help you to trust not just mind-knowing but also body-knowing. Any kind of pleasing repetition consistently done, whether it be movement or mantra, can help you to be inclusive of your body in a quiet way. And as you learn to be at home in this it will prove not only helpful, but comfortable.

Bodily postures that comfortably integrate you into prayer, such as standing in joyfulness or openness, kneeling in adoration or humbleness, arm gestures for supplication or thanksgiving, all help your prayer.

Gentle ponderings can calm and enlighten you, as can music that does not disturb. Favorite hymns, poetry, written reflections, or anything that holds personal messages or symbols can be a welcome or a solace, provided you let them draw you and nourish you, rather than probing them for your own mental satisfaction, as you might in more active meditation times.

When you are drawn to Scripture prayer, but find yourself untouched by a passage, seek out a story where Jesus heals, such as the blind man, the paralytic, or the lame, and place yourself in Jesus' healing power as the blind or paralyzed or lame person. Put yourself into the story. Let it become the outer form into which you can be drawn. Be blind before Jesus, who can touch you with his power. Or better still, be paralyzed or crippled in Jesus' presence, where the prayer can reach beyond your head to your physical body. In this way, your whole being enters into the power of this form of prayer.

Letting feelings rise is not too easy for most head pray-ers because the locus of feelings is the body. And yet, to engage in any or all of the above is to be open to feelings in subtle ways. One more fine form of prayer respectful of feelings is the healing of memories. The impact of hurtful memories comes from feelings around the event. To let them rise again, to accept and hold them, and to let Jesus be a healing power for them is a most positive prayer action, especially for the #567 person.

There are two other very simple and natural aids to your prayer: Breathing, and letting the steady rhythm of your own breath get you in touch with both the inner and the outer, and their connectedness.

Also, the simple beauty of nature can enfold you without engulfing you, permitting you a gentle self-remembering. Give time to it. The basic repetitive motion of walking in a natural setting is a contemplative invitation for you.

Perhaps all of these aids to your prayer could be summed up in words I already used: a meaningful lived (really lived) response. Find one that holds life for you and stay with it, let it work in you, let it free you from a narrow patch of thinking where you might want to stay and perhaps stagnate.

What Does Not Help

Obviously, getting into any outer form in a probing or unnecessarily processing way, or in a search for convincing data would not keep you in a simple, contemplative mode of prayer, if that is what you wish for. All your life you have relied on your reasoning powers to approach truth, including God as truth, so it can be difficult to put aside all the mind activity and to trust in what you consider to be less trustworthy. Be aware of this. Beware of piling insight on insight, or fact on fact, or data on data just to know more, or to pursue sense for sense's sake, just to have the security that you do indeed *know*. You will have to be honest with yourself and always aware of your overriding preference to stay in the head, to figure things out there.

Ignoring or devaluing images is another counterproductive mind activity. Images can come from the depths of the psyche and often let us know where we are or where we need to move. Since the question of "Where?" is the most active one in the #567 person, and since all your careful figuring out often does not really enlighten, you would lose a valuable directive tool if you did not respect and seek to understand the language of the psyche in unconscious images.

Perhaps, though, fundamental to any blocks for you would be a lack of trust in God. It might sound a bit blasphemous to assume that God does not really see or know or provide for my needs as well as I can, but, depending on the amount of compulsion, this assumption is at times held by some people in this triad. The author of *The Cloud of Unknowing* chides these people for intellectual pride in his *A Letter of Private Direction* (*Letter* 1979). Though he is addressing a young contemplative religious, encouraging him to follow his vocation to higher forms of prayer, his advice seems pertinent to broader and more basic prayer, and even, in specific places, to each of the three enneagram triads. On pages 46 and 47, he speaks to the intellectual pride of his young charge: "But perhaps at this point, influenced by the clever and searching scrutiny of your rational faculties—for they have no part to play in this exercise—you are beginning to wonder about the method and hold it in suspicion" . . . "My answer here is that your question springs from intellectual curiosity; and this will effectively prevent your consenting to practice the exercise, until such time as this curiosity is assuaged by some good logical argument."

"We Live by faith, not by sight" (2 Cor 5:7). The gift this triad is able to celebrate is a sight infused by faith into the gift of wisdom.

5

A Basic #567 Pattern

> Since 5/6/7s live so much of their lives within, the
> journey outward is their way to balance.
>
> (Zuercher 1992, 144)

The "within" that Suzanne Zuercher refers to here is, of course, the very heightened perceptual energy in which persons in this triad live. If you are one of them, and if the points of the last chapter ring true for you, you will find that discussion of the basic energy pattern involved follows quite obviously. Let me start by incorporating, in my own words, a specific clarifying insight from Suzanne Zuercher during an advanced workshop at ISL in July, 1987, and also presented by her in her book, *Enneagram Spirituality* (1992). I shall refer to this again in reference to the other two triads.

For the 567 person, energy and activity are rooted within, constantly filtered through perception and reasoning processes. This is pervasive and often unrecognized. If I am a #5 or #6 or #7, the world seems real for me according to how I *see* it. To verify that reality, I tend to perceive, understand, and collect data around it, and to keep at that activity until I am satisfied. The outer world is for me to take in and order in some way, to make sense of it, to put it in perspective. That word perspective is apropos because it includes the root word "to see" or "to watch," and the eyes are the chief outer sense of the 567. So here I am, with a constant ongoing activity in my mind, keeping me quite wrapped in my head, keeping me in an engrossing energy from the chin up.

The challenge, then, is to discover ways to move out of this engrossing trap, to balance the high energy within by moving outward. It would be a good start for me to accept everything outside myself as real for its own sake—a big order. Where to begin? Simply moving energy down from my mind to my own body is a fine beginning, learning to acknowledge its physicalness, its feelings, its impulses, and little by little to trust them as holding another style of truth.

Going on from there, to give an example, I could do such things as appreciating an uncomplicated rock, or a tree, each as its own reality, independent of how my mind sanctions its existence. Picking up the rock, I could let it tell me of its own truth through its hardness, its sharp or round edges, the feel and weight of it, the texture. I am reminded here of Teilhard de Chardin (an enneatype 7), the gifted paleontologist, who says of his childhood, "Then it was that my newly born attraction to the world of "Rocks" began to produce the beginnings of what was to be a permanent broadening of the foundations of my interior life." (Teilhard 1978, 20) I can let a tree have its own truth by touching its bark, handling a leaf, sitting on a root, and then respecting its being. You noticed, perhaps, that I stayed with the sense of touch in my examples. Touch seems to be important for a 567 as an immediate conduit for "getting in touch," for getting physicalness into balance. The rock, the tree, water, sand, etc., can be for me an effective meditation if I let it draw me out of my head into itself, that I may become one with it, and that I may hear and know its reality. Who can tell? I may be drawn to respond in a Haiku.

The power of the energy pattern here is to be drawn outward, to leave the mind free of itself, in order to come into the balance of wholeness. Remember the simple direction "outward," come to realize the outer as part of myself, and be in touch. With that simple inward-to-outward arrow, let's refer to Claudio Naranjo, M.D., an author and teacher knowledgeable in both meditation and the enneagram.

Outer Directed Prayer

This is what Claudio Naranjo, in his essay *On the Psychology of Meditation*, would call the prayer we have been discussing. His essay came into my hands four years after I had begun my workshop series, though I had learned about it and its contents at ISL. The book has been reprinted under the title *How to Be: Meditation in Spirit and Practice* (1990).

Naranjo approaches the subject through three universal meditation paths: the way of Forms (outer directed prayer), which he treats as concentrative or absorptive meditation; the way of Surrender (inner directed prayer), or trust in inner movements and the expressions that rise from them; and the Negative way, one of emptiness and centeredness. It was this book that gave me more words around what I learned from workshop participants, as well as affirmation of their experiences. So it seems good to share, as I dialog on each energy center, from *How to Be*. Naranjo does not correlate this book's content to the enneagram, so it was an exciting find for me. Nor will I be offering more than a few points from the wealth he shares—just enough to lend the weight of his expertise to areas of prayer relevant to my dialog experiences.

As an example, the following quote encapsulates much of what #567 persons have expressed in dialog on their prayer experiences:

> Just as our experience shows that certain poems, musical works, or paintings can hold our interest without being exhausted while others soon enter the categories of the obvious, typical meditation objects partake of the quality of becoming more rather than less after repeated contemplations.
>
> A Buddhist sutra or a Christian litany, the symbol of the cross or the star of David, the rose or the lotus, have not persisted as objects of meditation on the basis of tradition alone but on the grounds of a special virtue, a built-in appropriateness and richness, which meditators have discovered again and again throughout the centuries. Being symbols created by a higher state of consciousness, they evoke their source and always lead the meditator beyond his ordinary state of mind, a beyondness that is the

> meditator's deepest self, and the presence of which is the
> heart of meditation. (Naranjo 1990, 15)

The experience described may, of course, belong to any
pray-er, but it seems to be the underground stream into which
the #567 most easily and frequently taps, a reflex fundamental and familiar. This prayer mode seems to be the easiest to
grasp and understand as persons dialog, because outer forms
can be shared by all, a reality that is essential to worship and
communal prayer. This prayer form is, then, a good place to
start in our dialog.

Naranjo speaks of an external object or symbol as the
start and focus of this kind of meditative prayer, and offers,
among other symbols, the lotus. The center of the lotus is
empty, making the flower an apt example, because when the
practitioner concentrates on that center a kind of absorption
occurs, emptying the mind, freeing the mind's energy, allowing a quietness within the being. As we have seen in discussing
the icon, a person focusing on a symbol can, in a very real way,
become the symbol. Here is unity. Then the symbol can be
relinquished, as the pray-er moves beyond it to union:

> Absorption is all that we have enumerated: a concen-
> trated attention, a self-forgetfulness or self-emptying, a
> giving oneself completely to the matter or situation at
> hand, a merging with It . . . If the It be God, the experi-
> ence will be that expressed by St. Paul as "I do not live but
> Christ lives in me." (30)

A word here, too, about the word meditation. Naranjo does
not limit its meaning to performances with idea, thought, concentration, sitting, movement, or the senses, or with any other
familiar meditation techniques. Rather, he sees meditation as
beyond these, yet inclusive of them: "Meditation is concerned
with the development of a presence, a modality of being . . .
This presence or mode of being transforms whatever it
touches." (8) He explores meditation in great depth in the
book, and through a broad spectrum of traditions, east and
west. Absorptive meditation, in the basic way he presents it,
seems to articulate for us, to give us a clearer hold on, the
mode of prayer that seems basically connatural to the #567
pray-er, no matter what religion or tradition is followed.

6

Some #567 Dialog

A very enjoyable, and most informative, part of the workshops on prayer and the small group discussions that followed was the chance to dialog with the participants, to hear what prayer meant for them, who God has been in their lives. Of the many responses I have received in both spoken and written dialogs, in groups and individually, I'd like to share with you a small number and the few questions that elicited them. You may find them as helpful as I did in receiving and understanding something of the sacred and simple moments in the lives of these persons. I chose very few responses, but ones that reflected the most common themes shared repeatedly. I've left them in the participants' own words.

Question: "Can you share with me something of who God has been for you in your life? Are there some images, some special sense, some experiences?"

Some #5 answers:

> God has no image for me—only Jesus—and though God has no image I have, paradoxically, always wanted to see Him face to face.

> As a #5, I have always had secrets; that's a part of me. But now I am coming to realize that God is the one who knows me through and through and I really have no secrets from God.

> Early on, as a child, I came to know God as Protector, keeping me from danger, and also as a God who knew every part of me, as in Psalm 139. Maybe this was to heal my secretiveness; so even if I got lost, God was there to bring me back.

Sometimes God lets me into a Presence that is wordless and full of energy and light.

It is hard for me not to be able to see God when I think I am in touch.

"Seeing" is basic to this triad, but especially to the #5, so it comes through the responses fairly consistently, as does the honesty about the typical #5 secrecy before a God who sees and knows all.

Some #6 answers:

God has always been Jesus. Jesus was everything for me, an ongoing and rich relationship.

For me God is truth, and seems to hold the truth of who I am, So I always search the Scriptures to find that truth.

When I finally came to learn of the God-within I found I could do things I had not been able to do before when I relied only on the God-without.

God for me is the Presence within Jesus.

God seems distant at times and hard to reach. I often think of him as a judge—but a merciful one.

I want to keep close to God as an authority who is safe to follow, and who alleviates my fears."

God as Jesus, God as truth and security, and a God-without: these are frequent reflections that come through dialog with #6s. Even when these three enneatypes of outer-directed prayer learn centering or move on to forms of wordless prayer that broaden their God images, they seem to keep Jesus as their core focus.

Some #7 answers:

God is exciting! There is always more to be discovered.

I love the Eucharist and icons. They transcend images and draw me into the mystery of God.

My tendency is to think of God as Allness. "If I could know you through and through I would know what God is," as Tennyson says of the "Flower in a Crannied Wall."

C. S. Lewis said it for me: "When we see God face to face we shall know we have always known him."

I find God in personal experiences. Everything speaks to me of God.

I perceive God as playful, with an incredible sense of humor.

#7s seem to take the questions to a lighter and broader plane. But you will notice that these three types have, in general, concrete words about God, who is often "outer" for them, and who comes through clearly in Jesus. In the other triads you will find less clarity of description and process.

Question: "What about your prayer? Would you share some experiences, or preferences, or reflections?"

Some #5 answers:

It's hard for me to talk about my prayer. It usually means trying to find the truth of God in relation to my own truth.

Sometimes, through the gospels, I try to bring God into my human relations, in a day-to-day way. I'm always trying in my prayer to become wiser and more real.

I used to need books, but they began to leave me dry. Now healing truths just leap out at me from Scripture.

Sometimes I have the need to just sit with my sense of emptiness, just sit there until something comes.

Sometimes I can absorb the Scripture, especially around Jesus, and then be absorbed—that is, when my busy mind becomes quiet.

For me, the most powerful experiences of prayer are those times when I really get caught up into an experience of God that is much bigger than myself. I get there through the intellect, but it all goes beyond that. Those times of being part of the universe out there, of being integrated with it in God—those have been the touchstones against which I have been able to sort of orient a lot of things.

On a hermitage retreat, I was drawn to be naked as I prayed, in a desire to be known by God through and through. So, hard as it was for this very private #5 I did it each day, and it was very freeing for me.

As I listen to #5s talk about their prayer I can hear the probing mind on its quest, and the desire for that mind to be quiet and holy. The #6s impress me with the sense of responsibility they carry from their everyday world into prayer, and the solid place they make for it, with a faithful heart.

Some #6 answers:

> *My prayer for long years was just trying to be faithful to outer religious rules, and not so much faithful to myself. Prayer taught me to leave those "outers," and that was scary for me, but good.*

> *When I am under pressure and come to prayer, I tend to Bible-thumb; you know, I keep looking for the perfect answer, the full expression of all wisdom and meaning. I find myself looking through other books, too, to find it somewhere. When I can just relax, and not have to be responsible or in control, but just sort of let go and go with the flow, then something positive happens between me and God.*

> *Too often, I need a reason for going to prayer; like I seem to need a reason to do just about anything, so the Church's call to prayer helps me.*

> *For me, prayer seems to have to start somewhere definite, predictable; so I like Scripture or chant or icons.*

> *The spiritual exercises can be a compulsion for me because there is lots to do. Now I know I need to resist that, and just be quieter.*

> *My prayer was always trying to do God's will. I felt that would be the most efficient way for me to live. Now just being at prayer has come to be more important, to be there with ever-greater trust.*

When #7s dialog on prayer, they have an expansive tone, drawing much from the world around them, or pursuing whatever is at hand as a means to prayer. And they like to pray.

Some #7 answers:

> *Step by step in prayer is hard for me, as is just sitting and feeling the pain of things.*

> *I enter into God's center in prayer. He is a faithful presence.*

> *When I started to learn formal mental prayer, I tried to imagine scenes from Scripture—all in Technicolor—to come to know Jesus. But I spent all my prayer time making a Technicolor film, caught up in it, and missed the person of Jesus!*

As a #7, the idea of "more" has always been a part of me. I'd always looked to Jesus in prayer to give me that more, but at one point I was thrown into confusion when he seemed to say to me, "I know when the more becomes enough." To me that meant that I had to learn to let go, which I am learning to do, little by little.

What is hard for me is when I do not know where I am in prayer. It is hard to sustain that, but when I let go of having to know I have a certain peace.

I want to label everything, to make it have meaning, but prayer defies that, so it is good for me even in a natural way.

The Eucharist has always been a special place of private prayer for me.

One thing to mention here is that #7s and #6s often mention the Eucharist as a major focus for their prayer, the ultimate symbol and outer form. This point is illustrated well in the second #7 story of the next chapter, a story by Teilhard de Chardin.

Question: "Is there anything else? Anything that occurs to you related to these topics and your enneatypes? Anything you want to add?"

Some #5 answers:

Yes. I've always found it hard to get out of my secrecy and talk about my prayer to someone. Anyway, when I did, the person would try to give me a method to follow, and it never worked for me. I just don't like being told how to pray. [This seems fairly common with #5s]

When I read the Scripture passage on the woman with the hemorrhage, it reminds me of myself. I want to get Jesus' power and healing, but in an invisible way, from behind. To have Jesus turn and look at me would be too scary.

I like to return afterwards to an image in which I found God, and allow it to be nourished, like the image of water and its power. Often I can sit by the ocean and ask the waves where they have been. My dialog with them becomes a prayer.

Sometimes I even dialog with some part of myself.

Dialog is a frequent form of #567 prayer, getting thoughts into words that communicate directly, and most often the dialog is with God/Jesus.

Some #6 answers:

> *Sometimes when Jesus is not there, what occurs to me is his invitation to stand on my own, to do what I know I have to do.*
>
> *All my life, faithfulness was the most important thing, and the struggle to remain faithful. That meant following laws and rules and what was expected of me, having the security of tablets of stone. When God seemed to ask me to leave all that and find truth and reality within me, it all seemed so ephemeral. Now I do look there for answers because I have come to know that God is within me.*
>
> *What I had to grow in was trust, trust in God, and letting God trust me, with a sense that he is one who sees my goodness.*
>
> *I have come to the sense that when I can touch a place deep within me, I am in touch with a power that helps me to do things I wouldn't do on my own. Only gradually have I come to realize this is really God.*

The reliance of #6s on the outer eventually finds an inner balance, as these quotes reveal, and opens them to more inner realms of prayer, where, as we shall see later, they can be at home in utter quiet. As we move on to the #7s responses we hear people, as pointed out earlier, who are natural pray-ers, in the sense of being open to seeing God in many places and situations, in new possibilities and forms of prayer, and being willing to draw inward.

Some #7 answers:

> *The Eucharist has always been a special part of my spiritual life. As a teenager I felt drawn there, drawn to come to know Jesus as my Dad had. He was a daily communicant.*
>
> *I have always liked ritual and some degree of formality in it. To me, sacred place and time and posture are symbols of the holy, and a great help to prayer.*
>
> *Taize prayer attracts me. It has the things that make my "head" prayer easier: the icon of the cross, the words of Scripture and the petitions, the gathering into a simple liturgical*

*setting, the hymns, and especially the chants. I like the rhyth-
mic
repetitions.*

*At one time, I came to know that the mystery of my own inte-
gration is God's doing, not just mine. That helped me to let go
of wanting to know everything that is going on.*

*I received good advice about analyzing my prayer. It was, "Let
go of analyzing; just be with God."*

*Until a thirty-day retreat, I was afraid of repeating a medita-
tion or an image, dubious that it helped intellectually. When I
did it, I found it refreshing, found that I could go back to an
image and drink deeper of it each time.*

These quotes do not, of course, cover all the prayer experiences of this triad, but perhaps they will offer you a general
sense, and even a small view of some differences and similari-
ties in the types.

Moving On

Even within each type, there is variety—understandable if you
consider such things as Myers-Briggs typology and the influences of extrovert vs. introvert, sensate vs. intuitive, and
thinking vs. feeling. These influences are not under consid-
eration here, but I would like to point out some that I find
operative: the energies from the arrow direction and the
wings. Since some presenters do not offer these in their
enneagram teaching, and some do not even include one or
the other in their accepted theories, you may be unfamiliar
with them. For those of you who are, I'd like to close this chapter with a brief observation about them.

The enneagram circle has within it a distinctive pattern of
lines connecting three points. These lines, these arrows,
expand the basic energy of the enneatype, in general, negatively when the arrow points away, and positively when it is
received. Actually, both the pluses and minuses of the two

other types might be available to be worked on or to be worked with and integrated. But for now let's consider that each enneatype can experience strengthening from the energies of the type whose arrow comes toward it. So the #5 draws strengthening energies from the #8, the #6 from the #9, and the #7 from the #5. Let's look at this very briefly.

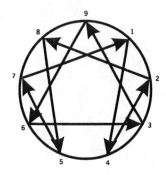

When the #5 and the #6 are in the strengthening energies of the #8 and the #9, respectively, they seem to have a natural aptitude for the formless or negative, as it is called by Naranjo, prayer of the gut energy center. If you are in these types, you may have noticed at points of integration in your life, or when you reach certain stages of inner growth, that you prefer a mode of prayer that is without process or outer forms, as near as you can manage it. If you are a #7, you may have used the #5 energy to quiet down from your multiple options and activities, and you may also have drawn on the energy of your #8 wing and its native preference for formless prayer of some type. Persons not actually in the gut energy center seem to bring their own flavor to such prayer modes as centering prayer, Zen sitting, or any prayer of simple presence to the divine, and these seem to provide positive experiences if the person is accommodated to it. As you shall see later, each enneatype seems to be influenced in prayer by the arrows and wings energies.

O Hidden God, devoutly I adore Thee, Who truly are within the forms before me.

To Thee my heart I bow with bended knee, as failing quite in contemplating Thee.

(*Adoro Te,* ascribed to St. Thomas Aquinas)

7

Two Stories from #7

If you are in this #567 triad, you no doubt have a knack for gazing. Perhaps it is so much a part of you that you are not aware of the gift in it, not only as regards forms of prayer, but in other forms, such as healing ones. The first of these two stories is from a person (an enneatype #7) who found this gift one of prayer and healing, and in a very simple way. Let her tell you about her

Healing Of Memories

A few years ago in January, my 87-year-old mother died peacefully of leukemia. I was in charge of the funeral, met with relatives and friends, and had no time to grieve for her before immediately plunging into a new semester of teaching at the university. In late May, I was on my way to make a private retreat, well aware of this unfinished business I must deal with. Just before I left, a good friend advised me to bring along any photographs I had of her.

After a couple days of inner quieting in a beautiful environment, I took out the little box of pictures of my mother. In the first one, picked at random, a tall young woman smiled down at the dimpled towhead cradled in her arms: my brother, who had died some years before. For a long time I looked at them. The peace she radiated drew me to her, the affection, caring, gladness. My mother: this is who you were then—still are now in God's presence. You looked at him that way, and you now continue that same loving regard for me and my sisters. There were times of suffering too: when one of us was sick, you sat up all night by the bed and we were sure you made

us better. Another picture: you were laughing with the
ladies you played bridge with . . . and another . . . and
another, this one bringing back a time I thought I had
hurt you without meaning to, and now I am again saying
how sorry I am for that. I know you hear me now and we
can talk about whatever I have left unsaid.

And so through many pictures, until a sudden sharp
knock came at my door. Someone peered in to see if I was
OK, because I hadn't been at lunch or dinner. It was night
and I was sitting on the floor crying, with photos all
around me. But I certainly was more than just OK. My dar-
ling mother had assured me she was with God, that we
could keep talking about anything, and she had left me
with her blessing of a deep peace in her presence—and
God's. (C. R. 1994)

The second story is a lovely illustration of the influence outer
forms can have on the prayer life of a person in this triad. In
his *Hymn of the Universe*, Teilhard de Chardin (also a #7)
includes "Three Stories in the Style of Benson," which he says
a friend shared with him, but the editor notes (41) that the
"friend" is Teilhard himself. All three stories involve prayer
and outer forms, but the second one seems to lend itself the
most clearly to what we are about in these chapters, and brings
their discussion, in a fitting way, to a close. You may well have
already read this famous story, but here are excerpts from

The Monstrance

The light was fading. I pressed a switch, and the lamp
on my desk lit up. It was a very pretty lamp; its pedestal
and shade were made of diaphanous sea-green glass, and
the bulbs were so ingeniously placed that the entire mass
of crystal and the designs which decorated it were illu-
mined from within.

My friend gave a start; and I noticed that his gaze
remained fixed on the lamp, as though to draw from it his
memories of the past, as he began again to confide in me.

"On another occasion," he said, "I was again in a
church and had just knelt down before the Blessed Sacra-
ment exposed in a monstrance when I experienced a very
strange impression.

"You must, I feel sure, have observed that optical illusion which makes a bright spot against a dark background seem to expand and grow bigger? It was something of this sort that I experienced as I gazed at the host, its white shape standing out sharply, despite the candles on the altar, against the darkness of the choir. At least, that is what happened to begin with; later on, as you shall hear, my experience assumed proportions which no physical analogy could express.

"I had then the impression as I gazed at the host that its surface was gradually spreading out like a spot of oil, but of course much more swiftly and luminously. At the beginning it seemed to me that I alone had noticed any change, and that it was taking place without awakening any desire or encountering any obstacle. But little by little, as the white orb grew and grew in space till it seemed to be drawing quite close to me, I heard a subdued sound, an immeasurable murmur, as when the rising tide extends its silver waves over the world of the algae which tremble and dilate at its approach, or when the burning heather crackles as fire spreads over the heath.

"Thus in the midst of a great sigh suggestive both of an awakening and of a plaint, the flow of whiteness enveloped me, passed beyond me, overran everything. At the same time everything, though drowned in this whiteness, preserved its own proper shape, its own autonomous movement; for the whiteness did not efface the features or change the nature of anything, but penetrated objects at the core of their being, at a level more profound even than their own life. It was as though a milky brightness were illuminating the universe from within, and everything were fashioned of the same kind of translucent flesh.

"You see, when you switched on the lamp just now and the glass which had been dark became bright and fluorescent, I recalled how the world had appeared to me then; and indeed it was this association of images which prompted me to tell you this story.

"So, through the mysterious expansion of the host the whole world had become incandescent, had itself become like a single giant host. One would have said that, under the influence of this inner light which penetrated it, its fibers were stretched to breaking-point and all the energies within them were strained to the utmost. And I was thinking that already in this opening-out of its activity the cosmos had attained its plenitude when I became aware that a much more fundamental process was going on within it.

"From moment to moment sparkling drops of pure metal were forming on the inner surface of things and then falling into the heart of this profound light, in which they vanished; and at the same time a certain amount of dross was being volatilized: a transformation was taking place in the domain of love, dilating, purifying and gathering together every power-to-love which the universe contains.

"This I could realize the more easily inasmuch as its influence was operative in me myself as well as in other things: the white glow was active; the whiteness was consuming all things from within themselves. It had penetrated, through the channels of matter, into the inmost depths of all hearts and then had dilated them to breaking-point, only in order to take back into itself the substance of their affections and passions. And now that it had established its hold on them it was irresistibly pulling back towards its center all the waves that had spread outwards from it, laden now with the purest honey of all loves.

"And in actual fact the immense host, having given life to everything and purified everything, was now slowly contracting; and the treasures it was drawing into itself were joyously pressed close together within its living light. . . .

"I heard then the Ave Verum being sung.

"The white host was enclosed once again in the golden monstrance; around it candles were burning, stabbing the darkness, and here and there the sanctuary lamps threw out their crimson glow."

(Pierre Teilhard de Chardin 1961, 46–50.)

#234—Let Me Say Hello

L et's move on, now, to the next triad, as the enneatypes 2, 3, and 4 introduce themselves.

Enneatype 2

Hello! I'll relate to you very personally, and I'll bet you find me a warm, cuddly teddy bear. There's nothing I'd like better than to make you feel good. Your every whim or need will get my attention because I feel so good, so energized, when I can do something for you, when I can tend to your needs. I really am a very loving person. That's my idea of a saint: someone who utterly spends self in the service of others. In fact, I am a bit shocked when others don't seem to want to be saintly, to give to others until they have no more to give. Don't they know that is our highest ideal? I'm glad I've known that, all through me, ever since I was little.

Some people tell me that is pride, that I am proud of my wonderful capacity to give—but others do need me! I have just about no needs myself, thankfully. Who says I avoid my own needs, or that it is a defense mechanism to suppress them? I am kind of blessed in being able to put myself aside. Well . . . maybe I do get tired and at times can tell my energy is being drained out by someone else. But I could not be true to my self (image) and say no. I just can't say no. What? I ought to try? It would be good to balance too many yes's with some no's? You know, at times I am put out because someone does not thank me for all I've done; or in spite of how thoughtfully I set things

47

up, someone does not approve of me. I'm beginning to see, though, how much I need approval. Do I depend on it? Yes, I guess I do. Pretty completely. At times when I don't get it I get angry, even hostile, and I blame others for not paying attention to me. That anger can even turn vengeful, and then I hate myself and I hate that hook I have of doing something good just for approval. Sounds manipulative? Yes, lately I've seen how manipulative I can be, all in the guise of loving and doing good. It's giving in order to get, isn't it? It's that needing to be needed, to be the rescuer. Sometimes I can see I am indeed deeply needy and dependent on others' approval. Sounds like I'm more in love with my self-image as a loving person than I am with loving persons, really loving them in themselves. Ugh! To say that makes me feel ashamed. And humbled. That's a different feeling for me. When I'm humbled it doesn't *feel* like a beginning to me, but maybe it really is; a place to start again.

Enneatype 3

When I meet you, you're bound to be impressed with me. Everyone is. In fact, I can sense what I need to be to impress you, and I simply adapt to it. I do this so consistently that I scarcely know I'm doing it, which says this chameleon feature has worked well for me all my life. And working well, or succeeding at anything, is the bottom line for me, with my can-do pragmatism. I get energy from doing. The more I do, the more successes I can pile up; and I have an easy competence, a real skill at organizing that always gets things done well, and means I will be approved, admired, chosen for top positions. I *am* my successes. Sometimes I coat my image a bit, or extend the facts a little to get a thing done, to ensure its success. Deceit? Exaggeration? No, of course not, just practical means to a practical end. I'm always doing projects, or organizing toward them, and I have very little patience with daydreamers. Time is money. How can they waste it? Workaholic? What's wrong with that? I'm comfortable with ambition and competition. I'm not a wimp. I even seem to have a Midas-

touch, turning whatever I do into gold, or a gold medal. I even
look competent and successful, like I have it all together. Of
course. I invest in myself.

People think I am good-looking, that I have a winning
energy. I know people look twice at me, and I make sure they
do, by wearing fashionable clothes and hair styles (you could
call me compulsed about my hair—it's got to be perfect), and
by being seen in the right places, with the right people. I constantly invest in my outer image, and it works. Don't ask me
about my inner self or my feelings. They are messy and get in
the way of efficiency, so I just pay them no heed. Depth? What
do you mean depth? Sounds dark and threatening. I have no
capacity for that. How about truth, you ask? I have, I think, a
buried sense of it, and know I'll be most myself when I can
swallow hard and be genuinely honest with myself, my feelings, and other people. It'll be a challenge for me to be quiet
and alone with my inner self, to come to know who I really am
deep inside. I've scarcely ever been there—I'm not even sure I
have much of an inner self, because I spend my time on my
outer self and organizing my outer world. You say I do have
that inner me, and that who I am is more attractive that what I
do? Thanks—I guess.

Enneatype 4

When you say hello to me and I sense a rapport there, I will
relate to you directly and warmly, hoping you will think well of
me. But if I sense a lack of rapport I'll be reserved, not willing
to invest myself in any of your negative energies, which I can
usually pick up. And I'll wonder why I came across poorly. I
seem to put myself in the short end of the feeling. And feeling
is what I operate on, so translating vibes from others is second
nature to me. Wish I could be free of them, and spare myself
those sensitivities. You know, I am even sensitive to color, so
the colors of what I am wearing and how they blend or clash
affects how comfortable my body feels. Does that sound overdone? I know, I tend to sound overdone often. If I had to say
what one thing most affects me, I would say beauty. I look for

it everywhere, which gets a bit unrealistic, even I have to admit. But ugliness is hard for me to take, and the world can get quite ugly, quite lacking in the elegance, the understated, the classy, the aesthetically attractive that I'd like to have there. And I often try to put it there, maybe by expressing myself in some form of art. Even though I can be shy of sharing my inner world, really sharing, I do it at times through music or drama or poetry or visual arts, things I can work at to be sure they are fine, not tawdry or blatant. I avoid the raw or the blatant.

Too much, you say? I guess so, yes. There's something in me that does not settle for ordinary ways of doing things, and I had to come to realize that I am compulsive about that, about not settling for how things just are, but always putting a new spin on what I do or how I do it. Just a part of the bigger compulsion that I am different? It fits. No wonder people think I am aloof. I don't think that myself. But when they chide me for looking sad, it's probably when I am feeling wistful about the past, or about some lack or inadequacy or anxiety. Anxiety. Now there's a bugbear for me, because it leads to two things that I do constantly and unconsciously: impulsive action and inner scripts. I'm into *doing* before I even think about or assess a situation, so it's often hard for me to just *be*, or to accept the present moment as it is. I want to do something about feelings or people or needs, and not let them have their own solution. And those inner scripts! I'm playing out scenes, encounters, anything, not only after they are over, but quite frequently before they even happen. A useless waste of energy, when you think of it, and useless imagination. People tell me I have quite an imagination, maybe a bit too active.

And if I seem a dreamer, I live with a sense of not being whole, of having lost, or never found, some very completing depth. When I am quiet and alone (and I often need to be—people just being near can sometimes be a demand), I can be aware of an in-built longing: for what can be, for a truer self, for authenticity, for just being real. Smile more, relax, be simple? Good advice for me.

9

#234 Prayer: Some Basics

We move now from the prayer that draws strength and resource from the senses to consider one that draws strength by being away from outer sense impact. If you are in the 234 energy center, you may have found that your tendency to move immediately into action or constantly make connections and follow them, mentally or physically, is a hindrance to your prayer. You want to come fully to prayer, to be there free of the residue that activity and over-imagination have stirred up, to drain them from your mind and body, but it is such a chore. How to let it all go, to be here at prayer, just here, just now, without anxieties or feelings or the impulse to *do* something? You feel pulled by the outer, and possibly by a restless body. The #2 can be restless to work things out for others whom they bring to prayer, and even, when they decide to include God, over how to help God about it; while the #3 can be busy setting up their surroundings and checking out their prayer to see if they are succeeding. The #4 may have a desire to pray alone, but memory, scripts of past or future encounters, and a fluid imagination do not leave them with a satisfying aloneness. In other words, you have a trail of distractions that seem to be part and parcel of your prayer.

Interpersonal Energies

These are strong in you, so it follows that prayer for you is relational. You are at home in tones of feeling with which you welcome a strong sense of God's presence, that seems to come through in symbols and images, Scripture passages, memories of past experiences of God that touched you, sacred places, beauty or solitude in nature, or places that do not demand the relating that consistently draws you out to others. These things refresh and renew. For you, approval from God is important, just as it is from others, but keep in mind you needn't put on an image for God, or doctor one up, or feel you are not holy enough. Put aside feelings (and they are *only* feelings) of inadequacy or lack of merit, or of not measuring up as you would like. These all keep your awareness on yourself and leave God outside them. Rather, bring them all to God. Settle into God's invitation to be present and to just be as you are, where you are, here and now.

Activity

A lot of it can go on in 234 prayer. Thoughts come spontaneously, seemingly with or without provocation. It may help you to catch hold of how much your mind, imagination, and body are involved in *doing*, and to let go of as much of it as you can in a simple way. People in your triad are very much taken up with the outer world in constant efforts to rearrange it: the #2 pole vaults into action to supply whatever might be lacking to the environment or needs of those being cared for; the #3 sees in short order what must be done to make projects or interpersonal relations move more smoothly and productively, and so, sets about it with efficient action; the #4 is rarely satisfied with how things are or might turn out, and reflexively sets mind and imagination to work to adjust it all to interpersonal or aesthetic "niceness." In other words, your mind, imagination, and feelings are invested in the outer, and your body reflexes follow them almost before you are aware that you have moved. Settling into prayer, then, can be quite a task. And this is how you might view it, as a task, rather than as time to be simply uncluttered and open before God. Freeing mind, imagination and feelings of their insistence, and the body of its muscle tensions geared for action, do need to be addressed, but you have gifts that can help you to let go of these.

Letting Go

One promising gift—as well as pitfall—is your innate power to image. You can see this at work so often in your concern over and ability to note your own self (ego)-image, how you look or present yourself to others. A deeper aspect of this same gift is the potential to look inward in prayer, all the way to an image or symbol of your Self. And you can put this imagining power to work for one of your most precious but overlooked gifts, your body. It is with the body you settle into prayer, it is the body whose muscle tightness and reflexes are still going even when you intend to stop, and it is the body that gets overlooked in your need to solve things by doing. So it might be well to attend first to your body, since it is no doubt the first and foundational place to let go of activity. And here is where your talent for imaging can come into play (and for you, play is a fine word to conjure re-creation), in any one of the many imaging or relaxation exercises or tapes that you find effective for you. Try to get ones that are the least "work." As you give time to allow your body to relax (note the word allow, not make or force), you may find, as it becomes your habitual way to settle into prayer, that you can let go of your busyness, leave it "out there," along with a number of distractions. Do be aware that some of your prayer blocks are physical, and be kind to your body, perhaps lessening your demands on it.

Inner Activity

When you have settled in for quiet prayer, and have put aside those driving tendencies to rescue or organize or reshape your world, you may observe them subtly influencing your inner world, or not so subtly coming in full blown. Surprise? Your nature is of a piece, so it seems these reflexes will remain with you until God's action absorbs yours, but that lies beyond these introductory prayer modes. You do, though, have some natural helps towards that transparency and unclutteredness you desire. You do not have to "work" at thoughts, images, feelings, or insights; they seem to rise from within, and if you trust them to come from God as you remain open to God, they can be nourishing and directive. In other words, in prayer you find you do not have to *do*, but can allow the Spirit of God to foster in you the inner movements best for you, and as they rise, to go with the flow, to follow the Spirit. This can lead to trusting the nearness of God, and so, to acceptance of life situations, to reality over imagined preferences, and finally, to the freedom to be who you really are, not how you image yourself.

Contemplation

For you as a #234, this centers around your very personal sense of God's presence, of that presence living within you, giving you a feeling of being at one there. Here is where you experience home, a profound sense of belonging. As you grow in inner openness to a trusting God, and in accepting what rises and flows within, you come more and more to know God as Spirit, ever "moving over the waters" of your own depths. Your life becomes content and centered. You can have a sense of God's love ever flowing, ever caring, pervading all things, adapting to your needs and ever personally available. As you allow God more of your inner world you find yourself becoming more present to your own unconscious, to its guidance and truth, to full awareness of your life reality, and to the Holy Spirit as your guide in all things. Your world within opens you to balance with your outer world, as your practice of contemplation gives you the stability to continue that balance. The core of your inner world, your deep Self where God abides, invites you to be aware of images and symbols, offered to your talent to receive them. Be receptive to these invitations to wholeness in God.

What Helps

Remember that your greatest help in settling into prayer is to lessen the urge to *do*, and to learn to just *be* in your prayer and in your life.

Preparation is very important to ease the body and let the mind and imagination grow quiet, to become present to who you are at this particular moment, and to how you are. As you settle into you, here and now, you can open that "you" to the Holy Spirit, to let yourself be led, free of your own willful spirit of controlling through doing. Restlessness may be your ego not wanting to surrender that control.

As Merton (a #4) says, "You have to start where you are and stay with it, because God is in you as you are, and doesn't expect you to be any other than you are, except that there is a change that God is going to make in your life." (Tobin 1983, 11) So come as you are, let go of the need to appear good or nice or put together, as if you had to earn God's love or approval, as if God did not see beneath the image you think you must project. Humbly put aside this compulsion and accept yourself as flawed, as "bent" as the enneagram wisdom says, and offer that bent self to God for healing. This is good prayer for you: to know that there is nothing in my life that God cannot touch or be with.

As you enter into prayer, giving your body the time and attention needed to quiet down, you may find it helpful to find a way to move consciously from outer to inner. Whether it be imaging or chakra exercises or yoga or music or muscle relaxation, or anything else your creativity chooses, guide your attention away from outer concerns and tasks to an inner quiet. Do this consciously and deliberately. Engage your whole being, but gently.

There is an attitude that comes naturally to the #234 person: thankfulness. An open and grateful heart seems a short-cut to let you dwell on the good things in your life here and now, and how God is an ever present guide and provider. It helps also to nurture your dependence on God and to release your anxieties around doing everything yourself.

Anxiety can also propel you into moving on, so quietly put the anxiety aside (when and if you get in touch with it), and focus gently on the present prayer moment, and stay with it. This will not be a comfortable place for long, as that compulsion to do or to move will surface, but the helps we already discussed will provide some refuge. The #2 will be pulled out of the present prayer moment by all the people you bring into prayer with you, a good thing in itself, and all the things you feel you need to do, but these are magnets that might pull you into the outer again. Perhaps bringing all these people and needs into prayer and then placing them in God's hands, letting them go beyond your need to help, would release you to be present to yourself and to God.

A #3 can find prayer difficult just in the attempt to move inward (introverts will have an edge here), and because your instinct is to check things out constantly you may find yourself shifting distractedly. Learn to let go of checking on yourself, on how you are doing, how the prayertime is going, on succeeding in it today, and trust God and your inner world more. Imagination will keep the #4 unsettled, following images and feelings that rise around past or future endeavors, so it helps for you to hand over such busyness to God, and to settle in, body and bones, to let God love you. (Try not to wince, try to allow it.) Merton's advice: "Prayer is not reasoning, it is intuitive, relaxed, letting go, collapsing into God . . . Have an awakened heart to cultivate awareness of the love of God, a continuous, quiet, humble desire for God." (14)

These thoughts lead into an important help for the #234 in the issue of trust. Because you have a deep-down experience of deprivation and insecurity, you may feel unconsciously that you need to work for approval or acceptance. You may tend to approach God this way, too. Better to approach God with trust. The reality of whoever and however you are right now as you come to prayer is how God accepts you unconditionally. So trust the positive experiences in prayer much more than the self-defeating negative ones, and trust that the movements that rise out of prayer are of God's doing. You will come to trust the images and symbols that speak to you more strongly than reason, the quietness and consoling power you sense, and the nurturing presence. You will come to see it as all of God.

Prayer settings that are comfortable for you will be of significant help. You have a sense for sacred space, for symbols that speak to you and center you within, for color and beauty, especially if you are a #4. Heart center people need a place that does not demand thinking or relating, as we said before, or one that would feed distractions and pull you out into your workaday world. Because nature is undemanding, you might find a place there of pleasing solitude, and leave all else outside. Space that is not aesthetically pleasing will often leave a #4 restless, unless you can rearrange it to suit. Simple attention to physical needs and space will assist prayerfulness for the #234.

What Does Not Help

Feelings seem to be a big item for the #234, a confusion of many feelings at the same time, unsorted, vague, and diffuse. The #3 may not always be aware of how much or how many feelings are operating. The negative feelings we already mentioned can turn you away from God into worrisome self-preoccupation, as can the feelings of not measuring up, or lack of worth in some way. Beware, too, of looking for good feelings in themselves, claiming the "success" of your prayer by the feelings it holds, or considering prayer without good feelings as not real prayer. God may have blessed you with a consoling sense of presence, but to be without it is not to be without God.

Analyzing is a real trap, especially for the #4, the over-analyzer, but anyone caught in the self-image concern of this triad can fall into questioning, comparing, checking, and a constant self-observing to see how you are performing. Then prayer can indeed become a performance. Distractions may be frequent companions of yours, and you will want to *do* something to eliminate them. You may set about this tidily and be prey to discouragement when you fail to control them. Better to bring them to God for safekeeping, and if they keep returning, "treat them like flies buzzing" as Teresa of Avila advises somewhere, and pay them no more heed. Try not to exaggerate them or their power of importance.

A common source of these distractions are the inner scripts the #234s spin out to assuage past bruises to image, feelings, projects, relationships, good intentions, and encounters, or to bolster future engagements of any kind. When you catch yourself sailing along in a script, simply call it what it is and let it go. It deals with the past or the future, and you want to return to your here-and-now present prayer.

Probably every one of these unhelpful activities is at root a by-product of anxiety, which diffuses through the #234 person thoroughly enough to be taken for granted, and so, often is not recognized. Anxiety is the motor behind your reflexes to action, to overcaring, to worry, to measure and compare yourself to others, to "perform," to project into the future, and so many other hooks. If you can catch yourself in it, accept it, and bring it to God as how you are "bent," as the enneagram refers to sin (not in a moral sense, but in the sense of "being off the mark" of your best self), and, as an offering of how you know you really are, God can readily accept it. You can, too, if you swallow a bit and laugh at yourself.

A Basic #234 Pattern

The compulsive deception that they are completely responsible for their environment makes it especially important for 2/3/4s to spend periods of time away from their everyday scene." (Zuercher 1992,141)

And the more compulsed the person in this triad, the harder it is to take a day off, to relax out of the constant motion and preoccupation. Have you found yourself not even wanting to go off and have fun because to have fun becomes a project? What will I *do* to relax? Where to go? Who to go with? How will I feel about it? All the scripts. Just to be spontaneous can be a challenge. To leave the scripts and the action behind, and to rest in prayerful self-presence can be a challenge for the #234. As we saw, you bring your very social nature to prayer, not to leave it, but to rest and integrate it in God. "Going away from others is only valid if it results in a quality of self-presence that meets the Divine there and flows outside again to other people. If it does not result in increased contemplation, it is merely narcissistic preoccupation." (142)

For the #234 person, energy is where the interpersonal activity is, "out there"; so energy balance will come from drawing on inner energy. If you are in this triad and have a strong introversion tendency, you may not have quite the challenge extroverts have, but the warning of "narcissistic preoccupation" is not less timely. In my experience, introverts in this triad have a distinct energy difference, though they tend to let extroverts describe the triad.

Your challenge, then, as you come to contemplative reflection or prayer, is to let go of outer demands and tend to the inner, to a very vibrant arena when you actually plumb it. In letting go of what others need or feel or think of you, you may find residual feelings calling for attention. Take time to get in touch with them; let them come into focus out of confusion or diffusion; let them surface and name themselves; and stay with one, letting it speak to you before you move away or move on. Move a bit slower; slow down your intensity. Take care not to overstay your visit with feelings for feelings' sake, as you may be inclined. Attend to any quiet within, trust what it brings.

As you let go of doing and overdoing, you can allow yourself to settle into being. You may need relaxation or centering techniques to shift your focus inward. Often during the day, you are psychically into the next place, and are unaware that you are not here, not present, not grounded. But in prayer you are called to face those "nots," and to be realistic about "stilling-down" time. Be where you are now, as you are now, no glosses. Whatever your feelings, images, movements, distractions, anxieties, incompleteness, just hold them there in God's loving presence, without questioning, analyzing, or getting at them. Above all, let go of any tendency to be self-accusing: "I'm not as holy as others." "I spend all my time quieting down." "What should I be *doing*?" Allow yourself to surrender, to let go. As you settle into the now, humbly and honestly, open to your deeper self, open to God. This self-intimacy, in union with God-intimacy, is the jewel of your prayer, being content in two presences: your own, open and uncluttered, and God's, intimately. You are there not to be quiet for quiet's sake, that could be quietism, but for an interpersonal presence, which is one of your prayer strengths. ". . . God is in our center . . . Real freedom is to be able to come and go to that center . . . The only thing that is important is this inner reality, for God preserves and is identified with it." (Tobin 1983, 13) Merton also says, realistically, "This business of constantly struggling to return to the center is your prayer." (16), the prayer of daily existence.

Inner Directed Prayer

Claudio Naranjo, in his book *How to Be* (1990), refers to this prayer mode by several names descriptive of its energies: Prayer of the Heart, Prayer of Surrender, and, as it moves outward again, Prayer of Expression. If you are in the heart center, you will recognize familiar experiences from what he says, and the different inner forms your prayer might take. Characteristic is the spontaneous movement as images, understandings, or felt tones rise from within, not predetermined but fluid and free. There is a receptiveness to what comes (including distractions) because the pray-er trusts in and is open to what often seems Spirit-led. Surrender is a frequent movement. As the pray-er touches into the direction God is moving her, she is often aware of it, and at the end can touch again into what it is. It is important for the pray-er to be in touch with her own spirit in order to distinguish being led by God's Spirit rather than her own. Discernment in spiritual direction will help here. Naranjo offers this view of what may seem to some too nebulous:

> In contrast to the directive approach to meditation, in which the individual places himself under the influence of a symbol, we find a non-directive approach in which the person lets himself be guided by the promptings of his own deeper nature. Instead of letting a symbol shape his experience, he attends to his experience as given to his awareness, and by persisting in the attempt he finds that his perceptions undergo a progressive refinement. Instead of holding on to a rigid form handed down by tradition, he dwells upon the form that springs from his own spontaneity, until he may eventually find that in his own soul lies hidden the source of all traditions. (Naranjo 1990, 15)

When this kind of pray-er opens to this mode of prayer and finds it native to herself, a whole world can open within her. As it does, though, external forms and images can lose power, as it were. For example, if you are a #4, you may have found it hard to image Jesus in a clear form, and may have long since settled for a vague sense of an image. Paradoxically, for people who are so imaginative, externals can be too specific, leaving outer images as outer, and not as inner "reality." #234 persons can find pictures, statues, icons, etc. (the very things that nourish the #567s) a challenge to relate to unless they connect somehow to the person's own inner movements, perhaps around something like a meaningful Scripture passage, a symbolically powerful prayer gathering, a hymn, or poetry.

As a #234, you may also have felt a vague unease with formulated words, such as those in rites. You could be uncomfortable at times of petitionary prayer (true especially of introverts) because such do not come easily to you. Head center people have more skill with words in specific application. For you, a given petition seems to have to shift out of the group to inner fluidness, be structured in some way, then moved again to the outer. Or you may get caught up in scripting the petition. In any case, it can involve unwelcome time and energy, and some sort of inner rupture. At the least, it proves uncomfortable for many in the heart triad, so they let others do it most of the time.

These descriptions may be freeing for people in this center who struggle for years to connect outwardly in their spiritual life journey. But for other enneatypes, who respect the surety and predictability of outer forms, all this could bring unease, to say nothing of real distrust. All the more reason for people who are in this Prayer of the Heart (and it could at times be anyone), to keep open to the Spirit of God and to have a realistic awareness of their own spirit and its limits.

Naranjo concludes a long and wide-ranging chapter with this insight into our world today:

> . . . Today we seem to be passing from a state of formalism to one of relinquishing forms and seeking inner orientation. Our culture seems to be at a point of transition where the old forms are dying and people do not want new ones but seek to grasp the meaning that older traditions have failed to express through excessive repetition.
>
> Humanity is increasingly aware of the prison it has built for itself, and individuals want to be freed from what they are made to swallow whole by their environment, Because of this, man's metaphysical drive is leading him in the direction of expression, liberation, revelation from within. (Naranjo 1990, 130)

11

Some #234 Dialog

I f you are in this triad, you may find you are not as forth-coming about your interior experiences as others, perhaps because so much takes place within, and the movements can, at times, be elusive. On invitation, though, you do share (if you sense trust) and do offer listeners a clearer view than descriptions alone can. The following dialogs may help, as it did many workshop participants in the other centers, who were a bit incredulous at first at what they heard from these people. You will notice a marked difference in response to the same dialog questions we posed to the #567s.

Question: "Can you share with me something of who God has been for you in your life? Are there some images, some special sense, some experiences?"

Some #2 answers:

> *God is my companion. There is a telepathic quality between us, just accepting of each other's thoughts and feelings.*

> *God for me has always been a gentle Father, like my own father, with a quality of bigness and kindness, someone who is always my security.*

> *I don't put a face on God, but He is there. There is a real relationship, a reality in my life that I count on.*

> *God is a mystery very real to me; but when I talk about it, other people seem to wonder if I mean it. Of course I do.*

> *For a long time Jesus was everything to me. I had a real Jesus-and-me intimacy, but now God seems broader, less definable.*

God is for me formless, but sometimes taking form within me as Jesus or as a Divine Mother. I have a sense that while God's presence is within me, it is also separate from me.

You may be struck by how different these responses are from those in chapter 6, particularly in their tone of interpersonal care, and their generally less defined sense of God.

Some #3 answers:

I feel involved with God, but I cannot capture God at all. I have a very strong sense of this.

God is other than I, but I ground myself in him.

For me God is a loving divine Person who became human and understands us and our needs.

God is hard to talk about, other than as an ongoing everyday Presence.

For me God is not so much mystery as Jesus, the companion.

I used to be afraid to approach God intimately. How to be with this terrible God, this Judge? Then the Spiritual Exercises gave me wonderful experiences of Jesus, and I met a new face of God, and I loved it.

Of all the types I find the #3s the least distinctive. They seem to have the interpersonal bias of their triad, but can sound like #6s, #7s, and even like #9s at times. Their ability to use images prayerfully comes through in their journey to God.

Some #4 answers:

God is bigger than my scripts: so enormous, but so caring, nurturing, and always affirming.

When I try to say who God is for me, there are just two words: Mystery and Presence.

I find myself not seeking God outside me, but welling up within me, and I can only let God be. This inner intimacy creates a sense of God as The Other, and even as universal.

God is like fog on the doorstep, an undefined mystery.

For me, God is a loving companion, deep within me. When I touch those depths, it is like finding a fountain which encompasses all of my life, and all of the world.

Simply a loving, inviting Presence; that is who God is for me.

God is a deep inner well, always drawing and nourishing me.

#4s do not seem to have clear words about God, but the felt-sense comes through. They seem unwilling, as well as unable, to picture God.

Question: "What about your prayer? Would you share with me some experiences, or preferences, or reflections?"

Some #2 answers:

> *It's hard to settle down with God, unless I can be doing something for Him, attending to God in some way.*

> *I can't stay with Scripture unless it has something to do with my union with God.*

> *The challenge for me is to leave aside what I think I have to do for others. My energies seem to keep going out of me, yet God seems to invite me to "come aside (inside?) and rest awhile."*

> *Even when I do feel I have moved within, I seem to keep looking around for what I should do now to make it prayer.*

> *Sometimes when I receive something from God in prayer, a peaceful experience, or a sense of God's presence, I doubt it is real if I have not done anything.*

> *Lately I have come to know it is good prayer for me simply to become self-present, and to abide there with God.*

#2s often mention that the action of doing some good appeals more to them than the more passive engagements of inner prayer, even when they willingly enter into it. #3s seem to take charge of their prayer time, with a sense of what is needed. Perhaps that is why they are more open to process for prayer than the #2 or #4.

Some #3 answers:

> *I want to learn not to make my prayer a project, but just to come as I am. That's hard for me.*

> *I set up my prayer to my liking, the setting, the particular Scriptures, and then I invite God to be there.*

> *It's reassuring to me to learn to start just where I am in my life. It lets me be self-present at prayer, and even if I do not have a God thought, I feel I have honestly prayed.*

> *Scripture is important for me, especially as it presents Jesus.*

Reading helps me to structure my prayer and to direct my feelings.

Sometimes I pray with a symbol, like the tree outside my room, and what it can teach me as it goes through the seasons.

As you will notice, #4s articulate more consistently the description of inner-directed prayer. These quotes suggest the naturally contemplative stance of the #4s when they actually settle down or are open to their prayer impulses.

Some #4 answers:

I bring myself into prayer, in from the outside, I let my body say how it is, accept it, and journey to a place deep inside.

After I have shifted into a prayer mode, I follow what rises in me, images, feelings, concerns, and bring them into God's presence.

I pray sometimes with Scripture and a candle, and sometimes I pray with what rises in me, and sometimes both.

I may begin with writings, or Scripture, or poetry, but then I move within and stay attentive to what comes.

When my prayer is one of real intimacy it creates a whole sense of God as Other, as "out there" and holding all things.

There was a time when I tried to be with God in a way that was not me. Now I come as I am, go down into myself, and find God there.

The times when God does not seem present, I offer my yearning for union with God as my prayer. That kind of darkness feels dwelt in, and is sustaining.

Question: "Is there anything else? Anything that occurs to you related to these topics and your enneatypes? Anything you want to add?"

Some #2 answers:

Guided imagery may be helpful. When images are allowed to rise up from myself they are very healing, and often help me get in touch with my helplessness.

I found that I could not hold onto the God of intimacy because then I would try to control and make God just my lived experience. Talk about manipulative!

It is still hard for me to own my neediness. Prayer is a real help there, if I can just sit with it, and hold it up to God.

Every so often, I used to offer to take over for God, to give Him a rest, and spend my time praying others through their needs. And I thought it was the saintly thing to do—praying my compulsion!

Notice the feeling-related words, which #2s use more than other types. You might also notice in these quotes the practical way of bringing #2 issues into prayer, issues of helplessness, neediness, manipulation, and the impulse to rescue.

Some #3 answers:

Nature is a kind source of Godness for me, especially if it is beautiful and I don't feel the need to organize it—like the ocean.

When I remain faithful to God and to prayer I feel myself also being faithful to other people. I feel steadier.

I like group prayer if it is done well. If it isn't, it grates on me. If the group is a smaller one, I am more at home, more touched by the prayer.

I have so much energy for life I tend to make a production out of setting aside time for prayer. I'd like to grow into combining them and just live immersed in God, rather than producing prayer time.

This last seems quite a wisdom plan for the #3. The remark about not needing to organize the ocean opened insights for me about this type's prayer energies.

Some #4 answers:

Relationships are where I can often find Jesus.

I love to be alone in nature. I have the feeling that if I could be there regularly I would become whole and close to God.

If I try to settle into prayer somewhere that is not aesthetically pleasing, my body gets restless and I have to move or change the setting around some way.

Silent prayer in a group is distracting for me because I seem to sense who is with me, and whether or not they are settled. They stay in my mind.

Praying alone in chapel or some sacred space helps me to focus best. Such a place lets me let go of my striving, of trying too hard, and lets me be open to God. I need such surroundings to release me for prayer, to be peacefully self-present.

I want to say something about when God seems absent. There is a way in which, though my prayer seems empty of God's felt presence, I have an inner conviction that God is really personally present with me, but beyond my own ability to grasp that presence. It's hard to explain.

For all their need to be alone when they pray, or to ensure prayerful surroundings, #4s generally do not separate sacred and profane; or rather, friends, loved ones, nature, aesthetics, etc., seem to be held as sacred, but at the same time appreciated as themselves.

Moving On

How do people in these enneatypes experience the influence of the arrow direction that strengthens them? The gut wing in the #2 (as we saw in the #7) can be an influence also, as this enneatype can borrow from it a more simple, grounded prayer style. Let's look again at the enneagram symbol and the trade of energy in the arrows.

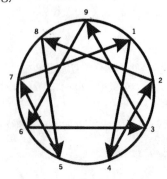

If you are a #2, you have lots of anxious energy for the outer, centered on people and what you can do for them. Like the over-involved #7, you find some inner strength in going to the quieter section of the enneagram, the lower part, in your case, the #4. Here you can settle into the type that is called the "contemplative" space of the enneagram, without sacrificing your naturally inner-directed prayer mode. You may have found, too, that at times you can settle quite soon into a simple being-prayer, from your #1 wing and its more steady gut energy.

#3 is the only one who does not tap directly into the gut prayer either by the positive energy arrow or wings, but seems able to settle down with the help of outer forms, possibly from the strength of the arrow from #6. As you become more at home with your inner self—an honest challenge for a #3 who dwells so much in the external world—you seem able to come to a much simpler mode of presence to God. Some big hurdles for the #4 are the lure of a rather creative imagination, full of images and color, and the trap of analyzing your prayer. Ways of transitioning into prayer and of relaxation will help you to accept the boon of imageless prayer from the arrow from the #1, as you will do in your own very personal way. Your preference for praying in solitude will function even more here.

It may be well to repeat that these are natural tendencies, a prelude to further gifts of the Spirit, hopefully, as these are gratefully accepted.

Two Stories from #4

For the #567 triad, #7s carried the two stories illustrative of the prayer of outer forms, and for this triad you will read two #4 stories around the prayer of inner forms. The first is from the story of St. Therese of Lisieux, her autobiography, and shows us a young Carmelite nun writing, as she was requested to do by her prioress, about her own life. The prioress, who is also her older blood sister, she addresses with the customary title Mother. Therese does not speak as much of the inner workings of her prayer as we shall later see Teresa of Avila do in the #9 stories, nor does she speak as directly, but in the more unctious nineteenth-century modes of speech, which, if anything, only tend to magnify her #4 feeling-based expressions. Therese does speak of a variety of forms of prayer, but in these passages, you will hear her say in several ways, though quite obliquely, the trouble she has with prayer around words, as many #4s do.

The second of these stories came from the desert southwest. During the six years I facilitated workshops in Arizona, I invited participants to share their experiences with me, or to send me their stories. Because of the vivid examples of the flow of inner directed prayer, I chose this second story. It (along with several other stories from that region not included here) shows the "natural mystic" tone of the #4, and the inner movements so much a part of the heart center.

St. Therese of Lisieux and Prayer

What an extraordinary thing it is, the efficiency of prayer! Like a queen, it has access at all times to the Royal Presence, and can get whatever it asks for. And it's a mistake to imagine that your prayer won't be answered unless you've something out of a book, some splendid formula of words, specially devised to meet this emergency. If that were true, I'm afraid I should be in a terribly bad position. You see, I recite the Divine Off ice with a great sense of unworthiness, but apart from that I can't face the strain of hunting about in books for these splendid prayers—it makes my head spin. There are such a lot of them, each more splendid than the last; how am I to recite them all, or to choose between them? I just do what children have to do before they 've learnt to read; I tell God what I want simply, without any splendid turn of phrase, and somehow he always manages to understand me.

For me, prayer means launching out of the heart towards God; it means lifting up one's eyes, quite simple, to heaven, a cry of grateful love, from the crest of joy or the trough of despair; it's a vast, supernatural force which opens out my heart, and binds me close to Jesus. I don't want you to think, dear Mother, that when we are saying prayers together in choir, or at one of our shrines, I say those without devotion. No, I love prayers said in common; hasn't our Lord told us that he'll be in our midst when we gather in his name? On those occasions, I'm conscious that the warmth of my sisters' piety is making up for the coldness of my own. But when I'm by myself . . . it's a terrible thing to admit, but saying the rosary takes it out of me more than a hair-shirt would; I do it so badly! Try as I will to put force on myself, I can't meditate on the mysteries of the rosary; I just can't fix my mind on them.

(Therese of Lisieux 1958, 289)

"The kingdom of God is here, within you." Our Lord doesn't neeed to make use of books or teachers in the instruction of souls; isn't he himself the Teacher of all teachers, conveying knowledge with never a word spoken? For myself, I never heard the sound of his voice, but I know that he dwells within me all the time, guiding me and inspiring me whenever I do or say anything. A light, of which I'd caught a glimmer before, comes to me at the very moment when it's needed; and this doesn't generally happen in the course of my prayer, however devout it may be, but more often in the middle of my daily work . . .

Still, I realize that we aren't all made alike; souls have got to fall into different groups, so that all God's perfections may be honored severally. Only for me his infinite mercy is the quality that stands out in my life, and when I contemplate and adore his other perfections, it's against this background of mercy all the time. They all seem to have a dazzling outline of love; even God's justice, and perhaps his justice more than any attribute of his, seems to have love for its setting. (218)

This second story was told to me as I taped it by a very shy #4, who asked to remain anonymous, except for her initials. As I typed it out, it raised echoes in me of Teilhard stories (cf. ch. 7), and seemed an appropriate complement here. On her request, I filled in the setting in which the speaker shared her experience.

Transfiguration Sunday

[It was a dinner invitation I had anticipated, and as I arrived at her home on a small lake I felt pleasure in the beauty of the setting. After a gracious meal we settled on the deck, and for a while soaked up the peace and lovely early evening glow around us, as it gilded the lawn and bushes between us and the lake, and set up sparkling ripples on the water. The trees closed us in, the sun silently dropped, and I was caught in the expansive quiet as she began.]

It happened when I was twenty years old, in a long period of thanksgiving after receiving Communion. That is, it seemed a long period. though it was less than a quarter hour. What happened was utterly silent but remarkably full. There was movement. At first, I surmised I was moving, that is, my awareness was moving inward and I was following it somehow, moving through a tunnel, or a funnel, very dark and getting darker as I moved on. Then I sensed it was not I who was moving, but the darkness, a contained darkness, was moving past me, measured by very faint seams of light every so often. What I call seams were so faint I do not know whether I saw or sensed them, but they were what gave me the notions of contained darkness within a realm of light beyond it, and of the movement I experienced.

Fear or hurry were not a part of this; there was, rather, a fundamental peace in feelings and time sense. The darkness grew deeper, into a blackness where the seams gradually disappeared. I began to sense at last in the intense blackness a warmth, a welcoming warmth. Warmth and welcoming grew as the blackness grew, and I could have stayed there forever. Slowly, very slowly, my awareness opened to a Presence, a warm, welcoming, unseeable, very loving Presence. What blessed me was utter belonging, utter peace, and the stillest joy.

For a while, I seemed to have reached a promised place, until I became aware that the movement had never really ceased, but was now somehow an aspect of fundamental stillness. In this deep dark, I was fully at home, and now I sensed rather than saw a pinprick of light far away. My awareness fastened on it. The pinprick of light remained just that, though I knew the movement was still happening. Gradually the light enlarged to about the size of a large pinhead, not much by our standards of measure. It never grew larger, but another thing happened, difficult to explain. There came to me the realization that there was too great a separation for any kind of awareness to reach that point of light, and yet, that was the same light that contained the darkness and movement around me. With that insight, an inner eye seemed to open within me, not unlike a zoom lens, and I could "see" far away a "window" full of light. The stillest movement in immeasurable reaches continued as the lens passed through the window enough to let me experience a split-second view of an ocean of light in which all creatures, all that ever existed, were benevolently bathed and tenderly held in being.

I felt again the warm and peace-giving blackness, and with no further movement, a gentle return to the everyday. It did not seem sudden because the peace and wonder of it all clung to me as trailings of my journey.

I went about my everyday then, thinking my experience had been a powerful glimpse into my nature as a human being, profound but nothing extraordinary. It was so quiet, so lacking in pizzazz, that I assumed this was just an ordinary part of becoming a more mature human being. Then, too, because it all happened after receiving Communion, I presumed it was part of spiritual growth, which I had begun to take seriously a few years before. Somehow I did not wonder about why I had not heard or read of such growth experiences, but presumed they were part of each individual's inner world.

It was only after years had passed that I came to realize what a pivotal few minutes those had been, and that they were not so ordinary after all. From my middle years, I can look back and marvel at the grace of it, at how the impressions never did fade, but became the lever on which I balanced many life understandings. I had a pattern, an inner view, of God as the Source from which any being comes, the same Source who surrounds and sustains all beings. I marvel at the idea of a person's being containing God at the deepest core, and that "in Him we live and move and have our being." (Acts 17:28) And, because the Holy Spirit had become of late a close friend and guide, it was natural for me to assume the movement drawing me through this experience was indeed the Spirit. To me the Spirit *is* movement, and wisdom, and the ever-present guide of my own spirit; so I was trusting and open, and knew it was good, it was God. Perhaps a theologian would disagree, but I have come lately to regard that darkness that held a sense of belonging for me, and the "warm, welcoming, unseeable, very loving Presence" as perhaps the presence of Jesus deep within me, with all his love and healing, drawing me to the Source of his own understanding of himself as God's own Son. Such a comfort all this has been to me!" (D. R., 1989)

I was spellbound, hardly aware that she had finished. The click of the tape recorder intruded, the lovely evening was over. I quietly labeled the tape "Feast of the Transfiguration."

13

#891—Let Me Say Hello

Now on to the last of the triads, and the personal introductions of the enneatypes 8, 9, and 1, drawn from their conversations, spoken and written.

Enneatype 8

Hello! You'll need to know I'm not big on chatter or small talk, I like to just say it as it is: black is black and white is white. I don't have a lot of patience with ambivalence, and I don't take to wimpy people. Just stand up to me, be forthright, and we'll get along fine. There is something else, though; if you are the underdog, or have been kicked around by people or by circumstances you can count on me and my strength. And I am strong. I have the feeling I can do anything that needs doing. That's been true all my life. I have limitless energy and strength and gut instinct to invest, yet I have a soft spot for helpless things, like little children, animals, the old, the frail or ill. People don't seem to see it, and very few ever know it, but I am just a teddy bear inside. Maybe I'm not at home with that teddy bear, because vulnerability or tenderness, or the feelings around them, make me so uncomfortable that I don't show them at all. I just tend to deny them if they are there. Denial is easy for me. I say "no" first, and if someone has a good enough case, I might say "yes," but "no" is my usual response. And don't be shocked at what might come after no, because I like the bite in words that folks call gutter talk. It's earthy, it's pithy, it says how I feel, and so it's my style. Don't get me wrong, I don't just chew people out, I have a fine-tuned sense of justice, but not a lot of finesse. To me life is basically hostile, full of struggle, and I have a sense of power over it. I like to take the other side, play the devil's advocate, and I seem to win my arguments—or I guess people back down. I'm used to that, kind of expect it.

I have a lust for life, a real gusto that never lets up, an ability to overlook pain, and a bit of the daredevil, too. With all this passion, though, I know my real balance lies in compassion, in the kindness and care it implies. I strive for that as a way to wholeness, as a way to interdependence with other persons, rather than power over them. When I find power and the lust for it taking over, I need to reach that little person inside me, the child of innocence that I am so drawn to, the "little child to lead me." Then the vengeance that grips me can subside, and the balanced strength that lets others trust me as a natural leader can really let me be the gift for others I am meant to be.

Enneatype 9

Hello there. I'm kind of a down-home person, so you'll find me comfortable to be with, if you like folks who are laid back and tend to take it easy. I sort of go with the flow (and in general I like a slow flow), and say what I see. Guess I can do that because the way I see is simple and straightforward, with not much room for complexity. Some folks tell me I'm too easy-going and don't have the self-starter buttons I need. I don't know. To me, most people make too big a deal about things, or are too fussy or too busy. One thing I've seen, though, is that, when others help me, I can get motivated out of my usual unfocused perceptions, and really do something, and do it okay. I depend on outer stimulants, and that can be a pitfall to getting hooked, even addictively, to what soothes or stimulates me. Wish I were better at getting in touch with what makes me tick, with my own center and my self-worth. But all that seems like so much work. True, I'm prone to be a bit lazy (I find that word hard to take because I feel I try to do my share), and to pull away from conflicts because they are so unsettling. In fact, I'm so good at that, I hardly admit I'm avoiding anything, I just prefer my own settledness. When that happens I just numb myself with something trivial, or with TV. I can be a real couch potato if I let myself be.

You know why decisive action seems to be hard for me? Because sometimes in conflict I'm frozen and can't see where the action is going, or what I could effectively do. Or it all looks to me like no big deal. You see, I tend to level things down to a small lump or a crawl, so externals will match my internal settledness, my nice, even, peaceful inner pace. But in big decisions something goes on in me that I really like. After I struggle with the difficulty and really name the conflict, then wait while I go on living my life, there comes a moment of simple, clear insight, a sort of combination of intuition and gut instinct, and I *know* what I must do, and often enough how to go about it. It is a special moment of "yes" for me, and seems to be the only thing that compensates for my inability to get things prioritized. I give everything the same priority, so it gets confusing, making it hard to actually initiate something or decide. I don't seem to initiate friendships, but I can be a steady friend. If I am your friend, though, don't let me lean on you too much, or for the wrong reasons, or expect you to do my friendship work for me. I really want to grow into giving as well as receiving what most appeals to me, unconditional love.

Enneatype 1

Let me introduce you to my #1 personality. You'll find me very forthright, with definite preferences, and quite ready to say so. I'm not slow to let you know how I see things because I have a terrific ability to hone in on what's right, a talent I feel compelled to share often. It comes from deep in my gut, and I know what's right without the need to weigh it out in thought. Not that I'm always listened to, mind you, but down the line I'm often proved right, and then I glow—or maybe even gloat a bit inside. You see, ever since I can remember, I've preferred what is right. I was always a good child, did what was right, and felt compelled to act out my parents' demands. I tried so hard at this that I have a lot of should's and ought's as tapes in my head, even as a mature adult. Now, though, those tapes have my own noise in them, my own inner anger, and they have produced a hard-bitten inner critic. This critic is forever pushing me to do not only what is right, but what is better. I'm a class-A Mrs. Right, or a Mr. Clean in a very messed-up world. I often feel I'm cleaning up a mess: I'm doing the cleaning up, and whoever caused it gets the full brunt of my anger, indirectly. Oh yes, people may tell me I'm angry a lot, as I tell myself, but my view is I've got to react to wrong, to help to right it. Lots of this anger comes from life's injustices, from people not seeking the best or at least better solutions. As I've grown, though, I see that reaction as a cover-up to self-anger and self-resentment, an anger at myself for how far short I am of those ideals in my lifelong inner tapes, and a full-blown resentment at everything that has blocked my way, especially myself. No wonder people find me edgy and scolding and, often enough, a negative critic.

Told you I was forthright. And I'm also very honest, a result of wanting to be good and right myself, and not wanting someone else to find a wrong in me before I do. But you know, you can trust me to be responsible. Often I am overresponsible about doing what is right—there's that "right" again! I should count the times I use it. It's when I get righteous that I come on heavy in a sort of prophetic doom tone. But I feel so strongly about social justice issues, and tend to carry the world on my shoulders. I'm quite often in a hurry, with too little time to set things to rights; but when I calm down and clear out the negatives, I surprise myself and others with my very real sense of discernment. I can most often be on target, and can be a real help to others, if I learn to approach others with the sense that they could be right from their different personalities and perspectives. I've learned I do not have to fix the wrongs in life, but can help if I stay calm, listen, and allow God and time to have a hand in things. Someday I'll control my picky, edgy, harsh judgments before they are sensed by the nearest person, and will be a balanced, calm discerner, with the gift of serenity. My ideal.

14

#891 Prayer: Some Basics

The natural prayer preferences of this final triad are much simpler, and, for those in other triads trying to understand them, they are also a bit more nebulous unless there is some personal experience here. As a #891 you may have read through the foregoing prayer styles and found them a bit fussy, too multi-dimensional, too much like work. Those styles may be familiar to you, you may have used them, but what you tend to come back to is much simpler. It is prayer that centers in the gut, in the hara point. For your basic at-home prayer mode, you instinctively prefer not to use the mind with its thoughts, concepts, and processes, nor the heart with its movements, imaginings, and feelings. You prefer neither outer forms nor inner forms, but no form at all. You have a natural capacity to just *be* in God's presence, without process, structure, or preferred content; in other words, you do not come to prayer wanting to think, feel, discern, process, or even move. You want to just be there. In being there, you can quite easily be empty, centered, detached from the outer, and drawn to stillness and unclutteredness. In this emptiness of sound, image, feeling, or thought you can be at peace, you can experience settled joy, a grounding in a deeper level of yourself.

Two Worlds

Although you find just being in God engaging and life giving, you may need to develop a broader attitude, one that not only includes the here and now, but also holds *all* that is in your life in the expansiveness of God. You are an either-or person, so a both-and attitude, an all-inclusive perspective is a challenge. Yet, if you should get lost in some sort of nebulous union where there is no real mutuality, you may lose not only a sense of mutual participation, but of your own self. Whatever this may be, it would not be the simple, basic prayer form we speak of between you and God. In your ordinary decision making, you may be a person who likes to dichotomize in order, perhaps, to clarify something for yourself. You tend to prefer east to be east and west, west, the inner to be inner, and the outer, outer. Keep things simple. Even though you may mentally keep things separate, you understand best through analogies (something is like something else), which involves a twoness of some sort.

The separation of inner and outer, where you wholly invest in one and then perhaps the other, sets up a dualism where you might see both worlds equally but be fully at home in neither. Your spiritual challenge will be to bring the two together, as in prayer where you relate to God as present, but other. For you to hold God as inner but not other could lead to a melting of all things inner where you could lose yourself and feel that you disappear somehow. This can be a temptation. If you are a #1 you could strive to meld into God's perfections of goodness and right, while a #8, though fully aware of God as apart, yet wholly a part of your being, may be tempted to settle for less in the face of the unattainable. If you are a #9, you will be most susceptible to losing yourself in God because it can be so effortless, while relating to God as Other can be work, even tiring, when you just want to be, to be comfortable and accepted. There is, then, for all of you in this triad a desire for this fully shared being, but also a fear of loss of your own being, even to a melting into nothing.

Images

One way for you to expand to a healthy inclusiveness rather than a careless drowning in one end of a dichotomy, is to pay attention to your own images or symbols. Here is a way for you to bridge without laborious concepts your either/or tendencies. For example, in being present to God, you may invite an image of God to surface alongside one of yourself. These need not be picture images, but perhaps sense ones, where you sense God and also sense yourself, with a realization that "God is God and I am me, and there we are," as one #8 put it. Invite a union of separate persons, a both-and experience.

So often, gut people will say that they do not picture God, they just connect to the being of God. But you may have experienced God's being as light, especially if you are a #1, or as unconditional love if you are a #9, or as the strength of your soul if you are a #8. Whatever the images, they do bring together the outer and the inner for you. Though you may tend not to process cognitively (unless you also have a strong thinking function), you often set mind and feelings into a dichotomy. Images help to get feelings out, to objectify them rather than letting them engulf you. Or you might just dismiss them, unattended, to stir up confusion later. Images help to bring together the outer and the inner of your thinking and feeling without intellectual drain. You may be drawn to dance an image or feeling, or to draw it in order to let it connect its message with you. Or you may have a strong feeling difficult to process internally. A suggestion: image a large, flat rock, put your feeling as an image "out there" on it, then dialog with it (a suggestion offered in a group dialog). You may find yourself more comfortable with the feeling and its message. Whatever you do with images, they have to be your own. To try to use anyone else's is to court frustration, as when a leader tries to walk you through a guided meditation. Images for you are often your own inner connecting with your own outer self. A common one I have heard in dialog may be a felt sense of Presence, along with a flow in and out, which is somehow very still. Another may be an emptying, one emptying following another until you are fully empty and yet full of God. Still another may be an experience of the hands of God holding you, not seeing the hands but knowing the holding. Your gift is a direct knowing and you will want to care for the images and symbols which nuance it.

Some Modes of this Prayer

This formless way of praying has a long tradition among religions. In the Christian tradition, you will find a number of descriptions, some very ancient, which offer insights and helps. Chief among them would be *The Cloud of Unknowing* by an anonymous fourteenth century spiritual director, who, in writing for a twenty-four-year old disciple offers you a simple agenda for this kind of prayer, and also insights into auxiliary prayer energies. His straightforward message is:

> ➤ *"Present yourself before God"* without analyzing who God is or who you are [an engrossing question for #891s]
> ➤ *"Reach out,"* an active, other-seeking energy
> ➤ *"With naked intent,"* which assumes a strong desire, not an over-passive letting be
> ➤ *"Toward God,"* with whom you are intentionally engaged. *(The Cloud* 1973, ch. 7)

Some people in this triad can view God as an impersonal force, or as amorphous, if you have a tendency to disengage or to be non-specific. Whatever your view, some descriptions in *The Cloud* will be appealing and quite helpful.

Recently the practice of centering prayer has come into its own, engagingly presented by Thomas Keating, O.S.B., and Basil Pennington, O.S.B. Many of you would already be quite familiar with this prayer because of its appeal to #891s especially, and to your preference for little or no content. There are processes for entering this prayer and for helping all persons to move to their center and to the indwelling God, but the appeal to you personally would be a simple presence, no processes, no words. Again, the caution would be for you to be fully present before God, as in Psalm 139, where the psalmist is drawn into God's own power and fullness, not caught in a vague sort of bliss, like a warm down quilt. The beauty of centering prayer is its simplicity, adaptable to all pray-ers, and essentially formless.

Another very fine style of formless prayer, and no doubt also familiar to many of you, is Zen meditation. Meditation here is not the mental pondering we associate so often with that word, but a letting be, and letting your thoughts be, without control or worry, or even impact. Here you are simply present to the universe, and to God as the great Ground of Being and Source of life. For you, this prayer is a way out of your dichotomies of right/wrong, yes/no, and such, because it allows that whatever is, is, without editing. Here is a vessel for the emptiness you are drawn to, and through it to the fullness of wisdom and of God's presence.

Of course, though you have a natural ability for these three prayer forms, their continued practice leads to freedom, but also invites a guide and consistent application and further study. Some of you in this triad may also have been drawn to the ancient monastic practice of Lectio Divina, the quiet pondering of the Word in some form, especially the Scriptures. You would probably not be interested in long passages in your prayer, but in perhaps a phrase or a short passage, repeated over and over, as if you were peacefully chewing or digesting inspiration. And then silence.

These are only some of the modes of basically formless prayer, but they tell us of centuries of revered practice, and of hope and encouragement. "Encouraged" is a word I hear many times from people in this triad when they learn they are not alone, when they learn they do not have to "make up things about prayer to tell my retreat director," because prayer for them was so difficult to describe. When they come to know their personal prayer energies, they know better how to share them.

Genuine Effects of this Prayer

If dichotomies have been reconciled, you may have experienced a profound oneness within your own being and in God. This leads to a grounding of your person, a stability, a not being caught in the swing of either/or. Now you can open up to what is happening—a centering of your knowing, feeling, and spirit. A sense of freedom allows you to let go of the issue of control, one that occupies you fairly constantly, and allows you to let go within yourself, and let God be God. Within the prayer experience, you may sense an open peace and a nourishing stillness that invites you to remain as you are in God for the length of the prayer. There is often a profound acceptance of what your life holds, of how God is guiding you, and finally—the nadir of your prayer—surrender.

Contemplation

For your instinctual gut energy, contemplation is different from that of the head and heart energy people. Without forms, feelings, movements, or processes, your contemplative prayer is a grounding in God, a being at one there, a simple existing in God. You experience God as the very ground of your being, in whom you exist, the Source, Mother, Father, of all that you are. You are able to simply let go, to be, and to be in union with Being. This is the way of detachment, of emptying yourself, especially of controls, activities, perceptions. This is the negative way of coming clear in darkness, in silence, and in the absence of knowing. There is a profound experience of joy and harmony in this emptiness.

What Helps

A major help for you would be to face honestly and directly the issue of power in your life, and how it seeps into your prayer. You are a person who tends to control reality in some way, especially your own environment, the situation you find yourself in, and the persons involved. This control can escalate to power concerns that will pull you up short when you try to pray with any openness. Your life struggle with either/or, fight/flight, you/me, etc., can be counter-productive with God. Your native negative prayer, humbly engaged in, will give you an arena to face up to and balance out the pull to power.

As the tendency to control is faced, you may allow yourself with God to be dependent and depended on, that is, both of them, not just either. This will help you to bring mutuality into both your divine and human relations. You will want to grow in constancy about this, and not just let yourself flip between a passionate drive for union and the indifference that says, "I don't care," a clear-cut "no" to involvement.

Conversion may be helped greatly by a further consequence of facing your issues of control—letting God be enabled in your life. It is like your ability to enable another to be her own power, to use for herself the energies you have not usurped. So letting God be and act as God, and letting others do so for themselves, too, means for you respecting another's self-empowering. Here is the nurturing that is a part of your best self, a refusal to be possessive.

The issue of control/surrender rises, perhaps quite often, between you and God. They are both there for you, so to keep them together instead of separate might mean the surrender of control. This is not the melting you fear, the loss of being. There need be no fear of losing your existence, but rather a letting go into the ocean of God. He is a both/and, both God and you, willingly mutual.

Focusing on a feeling—I am not referring here to Eugene Gendlin's focusing techniques (Gendlin, 1982), although they would be a fine reference—is a help for you to keep even-tempered. One strong feeling can take over your good intentions and de-stabilize you. Whatever the source or strength of the feeling or emotion, you would do well to focus on what it is about, attending to it as calmly as you can, with the thought "I *have* emotions, but I *am not* my emotions." (Assagioli 1965, 118) Feelings hold truths that they want us to become aware of, truths needed for healing and integration. When you give them attention—your honest focus—they can resolve, helping you to regain balance, to center yourself.

Again, imaging is helpful in giving feelings an arena for resolution, as was discussed earlier. Using images from your own dreams in clay work, drawing, painting, acting or dancing an image, or self-guided imagery to give a context, are all helpful tools. Simply splashing color on a page can be a strong expression. Journaling, especially, helps to extend the process or image, is easy to get back to later, and is a specific articulation of grounding. Heed your image, probe what it does for you, and you will not discard it.

Teresa of Avila (a social sub-type #9 with a strong #8 wing) worked naturally with her images and sub-images, and in them often addressed #891 issues of effort, energy, and letting go of fight and struggle. She worked from powerful symbols, as I shall discuss in the next chapter. If a symbol comes to you, harbor it, let it have its own life. If you are a #1, your symbol may call you to serenity, if a #9, your symbol may speak to you of your own essence, or for a #8, yours may be an invitation to innocence and compassion.

Another help could be nature. Enjoying it and just letting yourself be in it could aid you in realizing yourself as part of the whole, as immersed and connected. Cosmically, you are "here," a sense that appeals to your existential preferences, and to healing and centering.

And you will find more of your own helps to prayer.

What Does Not Help

Negative activity in prayer does not help. You are prone to judge, or to prejudge, so you may judge your prayer as lacking content, or as not being what you would like it to be. Be gentle with yourself. When you observe your prayer judgmentally, you distance yourself from the mutual immersion true to this prayer.

Your natural drive for union is a trap as well as a gift. You may try to avoid union by investing in a cause or another person, something that will allow you to lose yourself in the bigger or better without surrender to God. Be aware when you are tempted to side-step prayerful union or to substitute other consuming energies.

When you split your energies of gut and head, you tend to come through the head, something that St. Augustine used to keep his self-perceived "badness" at bay. This split can surely lessen your connectedness, until you bring your heart energies into the rift. Here the heart will unite head and gut and help to open you to prayer.

One of your important attractions, surrender, can also be a trap, especially for a #9. "Do I surrender or not? Do I, don't

I?" "If I get caught in the struggle, I lose God. If I don't struggle, I am not strong." "Will I disappear?" All this is unhelpful, and perhaps could be addressed by choosing some practical ways to deal with the dualism, conflict, and self-punishing mindsets that can hook you.

Any attitudes of judging, criticism, struggle, or negativity, rather than accepting, set you against your better, more prayerful self. Go easy. Again, a little less control, a little more awareness of interdependence and receptivity.

A Basic #891 Pattern

> The image for spiritual growth in the 8/9/1 space is
> one of dissolving boundaries . . . As always for the 8/9/1,
> the answer is not either/or but a synthesis of the two.
>
> (Zuercher 1992, 97)

The basic energy pattern for the 891 does not empha-
size what is outer or inner, but feels pulled by both, so
that this is a struggle. The freedom of "dissolving
boundaries" and of being inclusive instead of separating out
can lead to prayer that is free and fully embraced, allowing a
healthy being-ness in God. Any needs to know, to control, to
"cop out" are all left behind. There is an allness, a oneness, a
resolution of struggle and dichotomy.

If you are a #8, you may feel there is too much talk of
polarities. Your energy might be described by the word
strong, and you sense that you have the strength to carry
opposites together, to hold them as one, to minimize the challenge. "I don't say I pray, I simply live and work my prayer"
was one #8's response to me. Another one offered, "I don't go
in and out, or drop in and out of God's presence. All of me is
involved all the time, so I don't separate my activity from presence to God." God is so real for such #8s that one was
"amazed when I heard a person say he felt he lost God when
he lost his image of God. I was just amazed. God is a presence,
God is in all and all is in God. How do you really lose that?"
Your God source, though all-pervading, seems to be some-
what undefined, "Maybe like the sun. It pervades everything,

and I just want to be there, immersed in it." Struggle for you is not something you sidestep often, but usually step up to, and the questions raised by it are invited into your life, to be lived with. These are all things I hear from you #8s.

#1s and #9s, you seem more intimidated by the either/or, more challenged by the work of synthesizing the two. You seem more caught in Suzanne Zuercher's "When they see one aspect of something, its opposite is forgotten; this opposite falls out of experience and, therefore, existence for them." (99) As a #1, you live making comparisons of worse/better/best, and struggling with your inner critic about everyday endeavors. You seem to desire letting go of your critical push, the drive to improve yourself and others, and the often uncompromising inner demands for moral goodness. All this is a burden when you come to prayer. You may feel that you come from outside, from a self-adjudged sinfulness which separates you from God, and that you could get caught in a checklist of worthiness. This keeps your focus on yourself, rather than on God, and makes it hard to come to the simple openness you desire. You seem to want to "just be" in prayer, to find wonder and awe in God's presence, to put aside activity or the need to sponge away sin before you come to God, but rather to let God do it. When you settle in, prayer becomes simply being there in God, a relief and contrast, a redeeming balance in your life. You may agree with this from a #1: "When I have a sense of being held in God, then I can stop fighting and trying so hard." And for another #1, "God becomes the all-embracing circle into which I bring the pulls and struggles and contradictions of my life. They are all there, inside the circle, where it all becomes one, and I am one in God."

Union and harmony are themes you dwell on often if you are a #9—the hopeful results of the peace you hold as paramount in your life. But union, harmony, real peace imply a resolving of energies, perhaps a reconciling of opposites or fuzzy distinctions. "Dissolving boundaries" is not just dissolving, period, but dealing with the realities opened out. You may have found in your prayer that it is not always easy to be as aware of God as of the peace and settledness you enjoy.

Naranjo says that #9s need to beware of forgetfulness in essentials (Naranjo 1990, ch. 9), and who is more essential to your prayer than God? Your way of being open to God may be full of peace, but let it also be full of trust, trust in God's love for you. God's love, experienced as unconditional, experienced as mutuality, is your true resolution of dual energies.

Some Helps from Teresa

Teresa of Avila helps us understand some of the challenges and gifts of this triad from within her own healthy #9 place. She tells us in her *Life* about her simple prayer beginnings and what did not happen: "For God didn't give me talent for discursive thought or for profitable use of imagination. In fact, my imagination is so dull that I never succeeded even to think about and represent in my mind—as hard as I tried—the humanity of the Lord." (Teresa of Avila 1976, 44) In a number of places in her life, Teresa tells of her inner/outer, either/or struggles, such as:

> I was living an extremely burdensome life, because in my prayer I understood more clearly my faults. On the one hand God was calling me; on the other hand I was following the world. All the things of God made me happy; those of the world held me bound. It seems I desired to harmonize these two contraries—so inimical to one another—such as are the spiritual life and sensory joys, pleasures, and pastimes. In prayer I was having great trouble, for my spirit was not proceeding as lord but as slave. And so I was not able to shut myself within myself (which was my whole manner of procedure in prayer); instead I shut myself within a thousand vanities.
>
> Thus I passed many years, for now I am surprised how I could have put up with both and not abandon either the one or the other. (p.62)

Despite her lack of "profitable use of the imagination" or her struggle with dual energies, Teresa offers a wealth of spiritual riches, perhaps most notably in her apt images. In them we can see inner and outer united. Her most famous examples are probably her analogy of the four waters of growth in prayer and her symbol of the Interior Castle. In the first, she compares stages in prayer to four ways of watering a garden, from the first laborious method of drawing and carrying water from a well, to using a water wheel with buckets, to irrigating the garden, to finally, the least amount of effort as rain soaks and blesses the garden and God does the watering. (ch. 11ff.) With this analogy, she leaves us a fine example of careful distinctions and helpful synthesis.

You in this triad may have often drawn great good from your own symbols, as they come to you and as you attend to them. You may, like Teresa, have been puzzled by a task facing you, and had an experience like hers. She was asked to write a book on prayer, a subject she thought she had already discussed at length in other books, and in her prayer for help, she received the remarkable image that became a most fruitful symbol for her and for all pray-ers. She said to Fr. Diego de Yepes that in a flash she saw the whole book in an image. It has become *the* image of the soul, and prayer, and spiritual growth, in the form of:

> ... A most beautiful crystal globe like a castle in which she saw seven dwelling places, and in the seventh, which was in the center, the King of Glory dwelt in the greatest splendor. From there He beautified and illumined all those dwelling places to the outer wall. The inhabitants received more light the nearer they were to the center.
>
> (Teresa of Avila 1980, 268)

So, like Teresa, do value your own images and symbols as good guidance.

Negative Prayer

Images, though powerful for you, may be infrequent or even ignored, but in your day-to-day prayer there tends to be a negative involvement in, e.g., emptying, detachment from all around you, and a sinking into stillness. You like to be attached to no-thing. This, in fact, can stabilize your pull to both outer and inner, your dual energies that invite you both ways or neither, and to a consequent loss of your center. You would do well, then, with the sense of immersion that arises from silence and waiting, and that leads to being grounded in the deepest level of the Self. Naranjo describes it:

> Still another alternative to the guiding influence of the symbol may be found in a purely negative approach, which is directive too, but only in a restrictive sense: instead of taking an object to dwell upon and identify with, the meditator here puts his effort in *moving away* from all objects, in *not* identifying with anything that he perceives. By departing from the known he thus allows for the unknown, by excluding the irrelevant he opens himself up to the relevant, and by dis-identifying from his current self, he may go into the aconceptual awakening of his true nature. (Naranjo 1990, 16)

Naranjo's insights are reflections drawn from long years of study of the world's religions, of their meditation techniques, practices, and results. As I will explore more at length later, though these three distinct styles of what I call connatural energies in the enneagram triads seem to be, in an image Naranjo offers, three separate angles on a triangle, they do share a core reality. And the unifying strain of the three lies in this last triad. Perhaps that explains why *The Cloud of Unknowing* has such a strong and broad appeal, although it was written from deep in one tradition—fourteenth century Christianity. As a closing to this chapter, here is inspiration and invitation for you in the #891 triad, from the author of *The Cloud*, as he writes in his other small book on spiritual counseling:

> My spiritual friend in God, see to it that you leave behind all the speculative reflections of your natural faculties and give complete worship to God with your substance, offering your own self simply and entirely to him, all that you are and just as you are . . . so that your contemplation is not distracted nor your affection contaminated in any way which would make you less one with God in purity of spirit. (*Letter* 1965, 26)

16

Some #891 Dialog

Y ou may marvel a bit, as a #891, at all the words sur-
rounding something that seems to you as single dimen-
sioned as your prayer. After all, you can be quiet,
reflective, still, even empty, at your prayer, and, conversely,
fully involved in activity when you are not. What could evoke
less fuss?

These chapters are perhaps an invitation to let some possibilities and consequences pass before your consciousness,
such as your will to control prayer and action one at a time; or
how an immediate and untutored emotion can take hold,
leaving all else, including God, somewhere else; or the rav-
ages of an unfettered inner critic. As in the other two triads,
and in response to the same questions proposed, here are
some "words around" your experiences of God and prayer
given by #891s in dialog, with their unique and quite distinct
flavor:

Question: "Can you share with me something of who God has
been for you in your life? Are there some images, some special
sense, some experiences?"

Some #1 answers:

> *For years God was power and force; then I met a retreat master
> who was in love with God as a person and I found I really
> wanted that.*

> *God as Father and life-giver speaks to me. God was like that
> for me, and then became more of a mother: God as Mother.*

I find myself wanting approval from God, even competing for it; so when I catch myself there, I trust in God as living and forgiving.

God for me seems to be life. It's hard to say what life is; just that it's very real and not at all impersonal.

God for me is life-giver, in whom I always am, as if I am in a Mother's womb.

I fell in love with God when someone reached out to me and convinced me I was lovable.

I have no personal name for God, just God, who is always with me, knows me, loves me, and is part of me. A given.

Some #9 answers:

For me God is empowerment.

God is a personal God for me, who speaks to me.

I sense God as personal, but distanced, out there.

God is a Presence who holds me.

I have total faith in who God is for me, but doubt who I am for Him.

I think of God as a living, breathing background for everything.

I have come to think of God as energy, in the universe and in me.

So often I have been caught between a loving God and what I thought at the time was a demanding God.

I often speak to God as Father, in whose presence I feel safe and welcomed.

Some #8 answers:

For me, God pervades all, and I just want to be there.

God is a Presence that envelops me.

Jesus is God as concrete.

I think of Christ as the Sun in my life.

A provident, playful Father; that is who God is for me.

God is with me—Emmanuel.

God is mother, a feminine presence.

As you see, your triad has fewer words around the experience of God, whom you sense as at once extensive and personal, and as the sure source and ground of life.

Question: "What about your prayer? Would you share with me some experiences, or preferences, or reflections?"

These three types seem to knit prayer to their very being, find a simple way to express it, and speak often of centering, surrender, sensing, stilling, and a few clear symbols.

Some #1 answers:

I don't have a visual image of God in my prayer, but I often have the sense experience of being held in God and by God. Then I can stop fighting or striving or trying so hard.

I "feel" the presence, the qualities of God, not God with a face or a picture, but like the old man in church who says, "He is there, I am here."

I just settle into God who is my prayer.

Sometimes I feel my prayer is a battleground, that I stand there dictating to God on my own terms, and know it won't work.

My prayer at times seems to open to light, and I rest there.

Light is a powerful symbol in my prayer, too. When it is there, I sense God's nearness. It seems to promise clarity later.

Sometimes Scripture or simple readings help me to center, and that centering seems my real prayer.

I accept what my prayer time brings, and just go with the flow—no good or bad feelings, just enjoying whatever love notes God sends—all through the day.

Some #9 answers:

I always preferred to stay with one passage, even when we used to say the office. I liked it better in Latin, rather than in English, which has too many words with too much meaning for me to pray with.

When I am with God and feel healing, somehow the past seems to come into the present, without process, and I find great relief in that.

Listening to God is okay, but being in active relationship with God is a lot more difficult.

When I pray for long periods of time, I feel a peace that seems to expand into nothingness.

Surrender is a problem. I struggle with ambivalence between letting go and avoiding the question.

My ambivalence is between aloneness and intimacy. I want both; so it makes it hard to just be present to God in a simple way.

At different times, God has different names; but now in my prayer, God is just Source of Life.

#9s express the struggle with ambivalence more frequently than others, and seem to seek a prayer mode that is more settled. You will notice more vigor and directness with the #8.

Some #8 answers:

I want to be first "in God" and then in relation to Him.

Intense engagement with God—that is my prayer.

I don't take to a formal method of prayer, but just being centered in God.

I don't have to center, I am there. Centering prayer is great; not the structure to it, though.

In a Scripture passage, I can be, for example, the person Jesus heals, but I experience it more on a sense level, rather that seeing the image.

I like to savor Scripture passages in my prayer, because they can touch me on a feeling level. Repetition does not do that for me at all.

Sometimes reading something short is a stimulus for prayer and coming to God's presence. It fills me without words and I am there.

I leave myself open to however God wants to be with me: in peace, silence, struggles, intense feeling. God knows what I need.

Question: "Is there anything else? Anything that occurs to you related to these topics and your enneatypes? Or anything you want to add?"

Some #1 answers:

Yes. I've come to see how pre-Vatican II structures really did a number on me and my relationship to God with all the ought's and demands for perfection "as God is perfect."

I now like to translate "perfect" as holy or compassionate.

It took me a while to catch on to the hold my inner critic had on me.

When I feel I have a lot of inner strength, I seem to slip away from God. I have learned that my weakness draws me to God.

Surrender or letting go of control? Forget it! But when I came to "blest are they who know their need of God," I knew it was right on.

Issues of the inner critic and control are clearly often worries for the #1.

Some #9 answers:

My "hook" is looking for love. For a while, I struggled with God as perfect vs. God as love; but now I am back to God and love and I hope a good hook.

I had to learn to pay attention to my images, not discard them, and learn to see what they could do for me.

I've had a lot of trouble accepting dichotomies as both/and, but my #4 sister helps me come to terms with them. She loves them.

A very healing thing for me is being in nature and being one with the cosmos.

When my prayer seems to be an open expanse, I am no longer afraid. I don't know what to ask, but I wait for God and try to truly listen.

I am aware when I say yes or no to God or to my better self.

Some #8 answers:

> *Images for me are strong, powerful, but infrequent. I like strong images like the Grand Canyon.*
>
> *Nature is very important for me. To be in nature is to feel the love and care of God for me.*
>
> *I have become more responsible, in recent years, for my relationship to God.*
>
> *Images like night, such as "dark night," are not good images for me because I am a dawn person.*
>
> *I have to tune out of others' images and find my own. Maybe when I feel all tight I can image myself as a palm tree in the desert, bound in bark, and then unbind from that bark.*
>
> *It has taken me a long time, but I am now more honest in naming my needs and in asking for God's help with them.*
>
> *Journaling is a way for me to discern and to accept God's messages.*

Moving On

Again, a look at the arrow energies. If you are a #8, the arrow from the #2 will offer you some positive growthful prayer modes, as you #9s will be helped by the energies from the #3 arrow, and you #1s by the arrow from the #7. Let's consider some of the helpful movements that come from looking back along these arrows to the prayer gifts at their source.

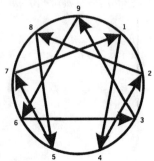

It has been helpful to me, in my dialog with #891s, to have them put words around their wordless prayer, especially the experienced shifts to heart or head prayer. Here are some excerpts from those dialogs, which will speak well for themselves, and be clearer to you than my comments. First, the #8 and #9 who open to heart prayer, then the #1 in the strengthening head center prayer.

> [#8] I found that this arrow theory is very, very helpful for me to develop my prayer life, because somehow in my relationship with God I can reach that affective level more easily than I do with people. And my prayer life in the past few years has been very affective. I pour myself out, I journal a lot during my prayer, I don't write about my prayer, I really write my prayer in poetic form. I make a lot of use of symbols. It's just a reaching out and overflowing that I find myself naturally drawn to.

> [#9] Aside from periods of struggle, my prayer was time spent simply in contentment with God—no thinking or feeling or imagination. Some years ago (I hadn't noticed it at first), I gradually became conscious of wisps of Scripture or hymns rising somehow within me during my prayer. I was not aware that my prayer might be expanding, but I did notice it was different. When I realized, as time went on, that imagination and feeling were growing into a part of my prayer I resisted, I felt it was wrong. I even became afraid of "other spirits," and asked my spiritual director if this was of God. After some assurance and a graced retreat, I settled in. I had known that enneagram #3 energies were growthful for me as a #9; but until that retreat, I could not understand how heart people pray. Now I'm not afraid of feelings and images rising in prayer, and can let them draw me into God.

Perhaps these descriptions may have some familiar sounds in them for those of you who are #8 or #9, or you may be freed up to notice your own prayer shifts and not be too distrustful of them. For the #1, the path will have a different set of turns and possibilities, as you open to what the #7 prayer preferences hold for you. Here is one sample from our dialogs:

> [#1] I don't have trouble centering, entering into prayer without activity around it; but when prayer is not so

good, I find myself restless and can even get into a battle
with God. That's when I resent God as measuring me—or
at least that's my inner experience, and I resent it. I've
been learning to somehow get the struggle outside myself,
usually in an image, sometimes even in a Scripture image.
For example, instead of being the self-righteous priest or
Levite, as I used to identify myself, I can become the
Samaritan and take measures to heal my battered self.
Then I can be filled with light and healing, knowing God is
very, very present. Sometimes it's as if God reaches out,
touches me, and draws me into peace, even a very physical
peace.

Of course, with the examples in all these chapters, anyone
could engage in any kind of prayer or prayer movement, and
draw great peace and benefit from it, without following the
patterns we have discussed, but many people have found
enneagram insights very helpful and enlightening by making
them conscious of their own prayer gifts, and a welcome
encouragement on their journey.

> . . . Rest in this faith as on solid ground. This aware-
> ness, stripped of ideas and deliberately bound and
> anchored in faith, shall leave your thought and affection
> in emptiness except for a naked thought and blind feeling
> of your own being. It will feel as if your whole desire cried
> out to God . . . (*The Cloud* 1973, 150)

Two Stories from #9

One of the great treasures in the writings of Teresa of Avila is the mine of experience and counsel in her books on prayer, all given in the homey style of the #9. Just about anyone who is serious about the journey in what she calls "mental prayer," will find pertinent advice or empathy, no matter the style or the length of the path already personally traveled. Of interest to you in the #891 triad may be her descriptions of her early prayer journey, where she seems very much the #9. I have chosen for this first "story," out of a number of possibilities, some excerpts from chapters 8 and 9 of her *Life*, where she shares her early prayer struggles.

From *The Book of Her Life*

When I was experiencing the enjoyments of the world, I felt sorrow when I recalled what I owed to God. When I was with God, my attachments to the world disturbed me. This was a war so troublesome that I don't know how I was able to suffer it even for a month, much less for so many years . . . So, save for the year I mentioned, for more than eighteen of the twenty-eight years since I began prayer, I suffered this battle and conflict between friendship with God and friendship with the world. During the remaining years of which I have yet to speak, the cause of the war changed, although the war was not a small one. But since it was, in my opinion, for the service of God and with knowledge of the vanity that the world is, everything went smoothly, as I shall say afterward. (Teresa of Avila 1976, 66)

The good that one who practices prayer possesses has been written of by many saints and holy men; I mean mental prayer—glory be to God for this good! If it were not for this good, even though I have little humility, I should not be so proud as to dare speak about mental prayer. (67)

For mental prayer in my opinion is nothing else than an intimate sharing between friends; it means taking time frequently to be alone with Him who we know loves us. In order that love be true and the friendship endure, the wills of the friends must be in accord. (67)

Those who follow this path of no discursive reflection will find that a book can be a help for recollecting oneself quickly. It helped me also to look at fields, or water, or flowers. In these things I found a remembrance of the Creator. I mean that they awakened and recollected me and served as a book and reminded me of my ingratitude and sins. As for heavenly or sublime things, my intellect was so coarse that it could never, never imagine them until the Lord in another way showed them to me.

I had such little ability to represent things with my intellect that if I hadn't seen the things my imagination was not of use to me, as it is to other persons who can imagine things and thus recollect themselves. I could only think about Christ as He was as man, but never in such a way that I could picture Him within myself no matter how much I read about His beauty or how many images I saw of Him. I was like one who is blind or in darkness; he speaks with a person and sees that that person is with him because he knows with certainty that he is there (I mean he understands and believes he is there, but does not see him); such was the case with me when I thought of Our Lord. (72)

It seemed to me my soul gained great strength from the Divine Majesty and that He must have heard my cries and taken pity on so many tears. The inclination to spend more time with Him began to grow. I started to shun the occasions of sin, because when they were avoided I then returned to loving His Majesty. In my opinion, I clearly understood that I loved Him; but I did not understand as I should have what true love of God consists in. (73)

Our second story is shared with us by a contemporary #9 pray-er who found the enneagram material helpful in understanding her own prayer journey, especially as her prayer opened out to the inner movements of the heart center triad, #234. She moves us here from her usual mode of formless prayer to a powerful retreat experience that left a lasting inner change.

There is a story to tell of my prayer, of a special time and a very special experience. Let me share it with you. If you are to be caught into this event as I was, you will have to know something of the setting from which it arose, something of the surprise and contrast that made the experience so memorable. So then, first, my usual #9 prayer.

For me, prayer is not something I come to, but a heightened awareness that I am always in God's Presence, and that now I sit at God's feet, absorbing divine love and presence. I am comfortable there, and quiet, ready to lose time in this very real realm of God. But I am also aware that I remain planted in my own world, with feet that sometimes feel glued to the floor, or, if I am sitting on the floor, I might sense a grounding, as if a pillar of light attaches me to the earth. Though I have no need of a preferred atmosphere for prayer, I seem to be undistracted by ordinary sounds: a car door, the wind, distant voices, birds singing, running water, and such. I am aware of them, but somehow detached and alert, with a focused consciousness. I am content to just be, to do nothing, to remain open to the contentment of being with God, always present. All else is left aside.

Well then, if it is true that nothing is needed for prayer, and often nothing "happens" in prayer, what occurs as time passes in this mode of prayer? The experience varies: I may have just sat down when the hour is gone; there may be a deep silence and quiet presence filling the time; perhaps a single emotion is felt, such as sorrow, joy, reverence, peace, even anger; or a simple message such as "Trust me." Or the whole hour may be swallowed up in self-absorption that is somehow still in God's Presence. This last borders on a common experience for me, struggle. Sometimes I struggle between a desire to surrender and a need to control, a very distressing either/or that seeps beyond my prayer into my day At other times, I struggle with a heaviness of body for all or part of the time, a physical weighing down that is not recognized as a major distraction until daydreaming or overconcern takes over. Sometimes my prayer seems so open, so without controls, that I fear assault by negative spirits or some form of self-inflation. Because of that, I resisted when my prayer started to open out to what I now know as inner forms, even though they seemed good and nourishing in themselves. My spiritual director supported me through this shift; so I was ready to receive, when the time came, the gift of Mary as:

My Mother

One day, during a thirty-day retreat, I went to my room to pray, and as often happens, I found myself quickly present to and aware of being with God. Generally this is enough for me; and if thoughts arise, I simply relate to them or let them go. During this prayer time, however, I found myself remembering a picture of the Sea of Galilee that I saw the night before. In that picture, there was a large log next to the water, and I felt I was there. In my mind's eye, I came to the water and sat on this log and, in doing so, I was facing the city of Capernaum, the city whose people had rejected Jesus' teaching. So, as I imagined myself on that log, aware of the movement of the air and water around me, I began to talk to the people of that city. I asked them: "Why did you reject Jesus? What was it that was so hard for you to hear that you could not listen?" Generally my prayer is quiet and simple. This day there was far more activity, but I felt it was right to be with God in this way.

Suddenly I felt God's Presence in a different way. I sensed Jesus (Jesus, not God, was a new experience for me) sitting on the log with me, looking at the city and listening to my questions. I relaxed and wanted to be a loving support to Jesus, as he often has been to me. Never questioning his presence, but simply enjoying the comfort I felt sharing this log and this time with Jesus, I let down my walls and completely relaxed with him.

Then, as if an audible word had been spoken to me in that room, I "heard": "Pat, I want you to know my mother." My response to these words was more of a shock to me than were the clear words themselves. My body stiffened. I turned, physically, to my left, deliberately turning my back on Jesus, and said in a loud, clear voice, "No!" I sat with my response, in shock at what had just happened, and embarrassed. The thought came to me, "What if that really came from Jesus?" Not sure what I should do next, I slowly turned back in my chair and tried to relax. Fearfully, I heard myself say aloud, but not as loudly as my "no" response, "If this is what you want."

In my mind's eye, there seemed to be a white cloud appearing. I thought that for sure Mary, the Mother of Jesus, would now come down on the cloud and speak to me, and I was apprehensive. The thought then came to me: "Was I to have a vision of someone I had never really understood or loved?" The "vision" I had was not of my making because out of this cloud came a deep sense of Mary's presence, but all I saw, or I should say, sensed, were two feminine hands. I sat there, looking at these hands, and saw that they were callused from hard work and yet they expressed gentleness and loving care. As I stared at them I again heard the words first addressed to me, "Pat, I want you to know my mother." At these words I broke into tears and cried for over an hour.

For years, I had wondered if I could be a good Catholic, because I never felt I loved the Virgin Mary. She had been unreal to me, a statue, sort of a cold, white perfection that I could not relate to; but since that day, Mary has been very real—someone I can love and identify with. In this graced inner movement, God made known to me his own mother, as a mother, a good Jewish woman who gently cares for me.

That happened a long time ago. My prayer remains basically simple, but now God and Mary are close sharers in my everyday realities.

Conclusion

In this closing chapter, I hope to leave you with just a few more helpful insights gleaned from groups and individuals who have found them helpful in understanding their own enneatypes and prayer energies. These are not areas I have used much in seminars or workshops, so I have too little dialog material to extend the topics in keeping with this book's conversations. Furthermore, the topics lie outside the formal enneagram corpus, more in the realm of meditation and reflective insights.

Let me return first to something that I trust I have made clear earlier in the book. We have all known moments of special peace, understanding, and closeness to God, and hold these as blessed and strengthening memories. We also have, hopefully, gained knowledge and encouragement from the masters of prayer, the mystics, who hold an honored place among us, and who are, thankfully, much more accessible to us today in our inner search and the needs of our prayer journeys. At this point, I hope you are more gratefully open to your own connatural gifts in simple contemplative practice, gifts that come from your body, mind, and psyche as it is uniquely configured in your enneagram type. Your natural prayer gifts are what the Spirit builds on in leading you ever deeper into your fullest prayer potential. But a word of caution. Along with your gifted energies are those that are contrary, as we have seen. You may find that you are guided, not only away from your compulsions, but even beyond your very gifts, as God seeks to purify you of what you consider "me," the ego self in which the enneagram says reside the prides and fixations. In this journey from self to the Self, in which, the mystics assure us, God dwells, and from which they share with us, you may find yourself called to let go of the clarity that your mind provides, or the feelings that assure you do belong to God, or the stability that physical and psychic strength seem to guarantee; in other words, deeper prayer involves purification. It is from this *state* of contemplative prayer, arrived at after a purifying journey, that the mystics speak to us. That is the point I want to be sure is clear.

When you read the mystics, you may sense the field of paradox in which they are at home, and which can leave us at sea. It is because their view is beyond themselves at the same time as they are very much themselves, that we can call on them and pursue their words of experience, and that I can quote them for some encouragement for you. This book is not about the mystics' state of contemplative prayer and being, but about the simple, hopeful bases of prayer gifts that we all possess.

Some Simple Ground Rules

A friend shared with me one day a simple formula that she used as a grounding for her own contemplative time each day. It fits so well with the three enneagram triads and the prayer instincts within each of us that I asked to share it with you here. She calls it her "Formula of the Four S's," and it seems to be a summary of some good traditional advice that you would have heard, perhaps often:

> Solitude, moving away into personal alone space
> Silence, especially of the inner mind chatter
> Stillness, for a quiet imagination and body
> Surrender, of controls and agenda

You may see right away how the last three fit the triads and their main challenges.

Solitude: All persons who hope for the best setting for quiet prayer would prefer a place alone, free of the distractions of noise and other presences. You probably have a favorite place where you can just be and be prayerful, but as we've seen, some people are more conscious of others, of movements, of intrusions, and need to choose their solitude with more care. No matter your preferences and challenges, for serious and consistent quiet prayer you will need a place apart, as Jesus patterned for us.

Silence: Oh, the busy mind! We all need the buffer zones that will separate us from our over involved lives and allow the mind to come to rest. But if your mind is heavily guarding your sense of who you are, as with #567s, you will indeed have a challenge. With the head as your center of activity and energy, you will want to spend your time there, in the mode of being that you trust and rely on. You are used to having your mind full and busy, helping you to "see" clearly; and fully uncluttered is not comfortable, you may think not even possible. And so, you can appreciate the invitations of such practices as Zen, and their promise of silence in mind, body, and environment.

Stillness: You may be able, with learned techniques or repeated efforts, to put plans or ideas or questions out of your mind for the length of your prayer time; but if you are a #234, your imagination is liable to take over in past or future scenarios, along with their attendant anxieties and feelings. And with these contents come the muscle tightness or action reflexes that can preclude a serene engagement with God. When these unwanted intruders have been accepted as real, here and now, but not dwelt on, there may be a chance for some natural stillness. But beware of any kind of forced stillness; it would at best be a counterproductive and subtle form of distraction, and keep you from, not help you toward, the divine presence. Some simple, healthy forms of relaxation before you pray might be the down-to-earth help you need to let your body and imagination grow calm.

Surrender: So many of the mystics frequently invite us to this, and though we may be drawn to surrender to God, too many of us cannot seem to find out how to do it. In a surprising way the #234s, with all their action orientation, have a capacity to let go in an inner way, the way that they accept and attend to what rises within them in prayer. This can, if they are open to God's guiding, lead to genuine surrender. Indeed, Claudio Naranjo calls theirs the prayer of surrender. (Naranjo 1990, ch. 4) The #567, in the outer forms that draw and immerse them, find a surrender and a timelessness in the fulfilling of their kind of prayer. It is to the #891 triad that the call to surrender seems best focused. As we have seen Teresa of Avila point out, the resolution of the struggle with either/or will not come short of surrender. The urge to control, to be on top, to struggle with the angel until he blesses you, as Jacob did, will one day give way; but if it is to a token surrender or if you deflect your struggle away from God just to be rid of it, you will not, as you must well know, find inner rest. How fitting is the #9 St. Augustine's ". . . You have made us for yourself, O Lord, and restless is our heart until it rests in you." (Augustine 1960, 43)

The invitation to all of us is to all four of these, as the Spirit draws us, though it would seem wise to spend some quiet time and thought where we have our particular focus of challenge. It may lead to help and insight.

Energy Centers: Allied to the above suggestions is another that you may find helpful, especially if you are aware of your body as it rests—or tries to—in prayer.

The main energy centers, as the enneagram reflects, are in the head, the heart, and the gut. Depending on your triad, you may want to get in touch with and open your own overused center, to release the stored up energy, negative and positive. Or you may want to open them all as a balance and a prelude to prayer. Many of you will already be familiar with the following simple imaging exercise, which may help a bit, and I would suggest another small step beyond it.

The imaging consists in "seeing" a tiny ball of light in the center of, for example, your head, and letting it enlarge slowly, until it fills your head space and clears out anything else. If you stay with it and let the ball of light take over, you will feel a loosening of tensions and a release from your mind's content, a relaxing sphere in which to just be. The same can be done with the heart area, letting the ball of light expand from deep in the middle of your upper chest area and back, as the muscle tensions give way, feeling pressures subside, and your neck, shoulders, and upper back experience openness and quiet. For the gut, image the ball of light deep in the middle of your abdomen, and as it grows and expands let your whole attention be there, let your whole body and its activities settle there. This exercise does not require your mind to work, but just to focus quietly on the expanding ball. Through such a gentle focus, and the implicit care of and inclusion in your own body, you may leave it settled and move on, then, to fruitful prayer. Though you may pay more attention to your own overused energy center, it is good to dwell on all three, for balance.

But this exercise is not prayer itself. It does, however, intimate a further step that could be a contemplative moment. The #567 triad, whose drive is to be the knower, often finds it hard to let the self be known, so a prayerful movement might be for you in this triad to open your head center, not just to know and receive God, but to be known, fully, in your whole person, to be transparent to and absorbed in the divine knowledge. You may find yourself resisting, quite understandably, as you let go of the power that you find in your own knowledge, but if so, you would have to face yourself honestly and admit where your ego is—and where God is inviting you.

For you in the #234 triad, the lovers of people, who engage yourselves in pleasing, doing for, or being sensitively conscious of others, you will benefit physiologically from release of your body's heart energy center, and you will, no doubt, want to rest in loving God in your own proven way. But it seems generally more difficult for you to receive love than to give it, so a generous movement here would be for you very simply, without fanfare, to let God love you. Opening the energies of your heart center, not engaging in what-ifs but being receptive to divine love and care, may "feel" like curtailment, or even embarrassment, but let it happen and the imagined difficulty soon vanishes. You will no doubt be relieved to find this does not require activity or project planning, and may well ease you into nourishing moments of prayer without effort.

Now we come to the gut, where the energies command the strongly instinctual. For you who invest in this center, one real challenge will be to resist taking charge, or to get involved with God in a bit of one-upmanship or bargaining. Even in the simple exercise above, provided you indeed do the imaging, you could set up your own boundaries and let in only "so much" of God; then you would be in charge. But instead of holding God, whether at bay or in some negotiated stance, can you let yourself be held by God? A challenge indeed! You are likely to sense a loss of control and self-direction, or awkwardness in moving into conscious receptivity, but that surrender itself will bless you, as Jacob was powerfully blessed.

All of us, indeed, would find each of these movements awesome, even though they were experienced in a simple way, but each of us could find ourselves in one of them, or perhaps more than one, if we chose that openness. The hope is to be realistic about our own energies, and to accept the blessings that would bring. Having the courage to allow God to know, love, and hold you in being is blessing indeed.

God's Invitation

In the enneagram there is a profound teaching that receives too little notice, and in general seems to be confined in group work to a list of noble attractions that will assist us in healing the traps of our fixations. And yet, these are the high points in enneagram study for those who seriously pursue spiritual growth. It would indeed be remiss of me to close this book without bringing them in; though, because I, too, spend insufficient group time with them, I have insufficient dialog materials with which to discuss them here. They are what the enneagram calls the Divine Idea, and what I like to call God's Invitation. What has often struck me is what a strong interior attitude they offer for prayer, a personal and quite specific still point, tailor-made for each person. This is how Claudio Naranjo describes them in the enneagram context:

> Whilst it is a goal of this tradition of work-on-self to bring about a shift in the control of behavior from the lower emotional center of the passions to a higher center, a still further stage is envisioned: a shift from the lower intellectual center of ordinary cognition—pervaded by wrong views of reality formed in childhood (fixations)—to the higher intellectual center of *contemplative intuitive understanding.* [Italics mine] (Naranjo 1990, 4)

In the instinct triad, the intuitive understandings that would infuse their basically wordless prayer would be, for the #1, a sense of letting go of immediacy in the energy toward perfection, and settling in with patience to patterns of growth; for the #9, a knowing of God's love as unconditional, as a sure presence, providing the verve for life's tasks; and, for the #8, an innocence that sees clearly enough to share God's mercy and compassion.

The heart triad, so given to movement, is invited to put it aside and to be quietly receptive to gifts offered. The intuitive grace of the #2 *is* grace, the free gift of God's love, not to be won by doing for God, but simply received, humbly. The #3 will know God's will as the real matrix of success, will pray from within it, and come to discover that illusive inner self they crave, there all along in God's will for them. The usually contemplative and intuitive #4 finds the source of that inner longing and the balm for any sense of inadequacy in the understanding of being called to union with God, and living from and within that call, both in prayer and in the rest of life.

In keeping with their outer-directed prayer, those of the knowledge triad deepen their own understanding of what is around them. The #5 finds all that needs to be known in what God provides, without an undue fascination with or collection of ideas, just a knowing of provident love. Security concerns for the #6 are left aside in a strong intuitive trust, not in what God does or requires, but in God's own protecting love, the ultimate insurance for life. All options for the energetic #7 blend into a single creative process, a quiet involvement in working, seriously and consistently, with the one Creator, and knowing the gift of this for others, even as pain and suffering become accepted.

These Divine Ideas are not meant as maps, but as pervasive intuitive attitudes for the pray-er, or for any person reaching the point of psycho-spiritual maturity where these can be freely and humbly accepted, and activated as potent integrating gifts for living an authentic reflective life. May you do so. And may this little book be of some help.

Appendix
Chakras and the Enneagram

Every so often, I have included in a seminar or workshop some time on the chakras as they seem to relate to the enneagram and the help they could be to the pray-er. When I have worked one-on-one, I have found that, unless the person has had the discipline of time and practice, the correlation is lost, and such information is not helpful. That insight prompted me to set this subject aside from the text, and just to add it here for those who are familiar with chakra work, and might find these thoughts interesting.

A Brief View

This material is meant more for comment than for teaching, so then, a passing, and only partial look now at what the chakras are and how some aspects of them may relate to enneatypes. Frances Vaughan, in *The Inward Arc* (1995), has in her descriptions telling words and phrases for our enneagram reference, and a liberal use of her quotes will make this section clearer and, I hope, more authoritative. "In yoga psychology, the seven chakras are defined as centers of psychic energy located in the human body." (98) In her words, "The chakras are said to be open when obstructions to transcendent bliss have been removed." (99) It is in this understanding that we find the crux of chakra and enneagram energies in relation to prayer. If we can find the blocks, we just might find that the body placement of our enneagram energy, and its conservation or hoarding, are aligned with difficulties in opening the chakras. Opening the chakras "is associated with becoming aware of the subtle levels of consciousness they represent" (99) and, perhaps, of much less subtle compulsions. See if some of the following exploration does not find a correspondence in you—and I call it "exploration" purposefully, since I can find so little written on these connections, especially as they relate to the enneagram and prayer.

Chakra and Enneatype

"The joy and vitality of the life force seems to emanate from the abdomen. The heart region in the chest seems to contain and radiate universal love, while the head region is associated with insight and intellectual bliss." (99) Do you notice and actually experience the strength of your enneagram center in this description?

First, where are the chakras located? Rosalyn Bruyere in *Wheels of Light* (1989) gives a concise map: "The seven major chakras are located along a central axis parallel to the spinal column of the physical body."

> The placement of the first chakra is between the base of the spine and the pubic bone. The second chakra is situated behind and just below the navel. The third chakra should sit in the V formed by the rib cage. The fourth center, or heart chakra, is situated midway between the two breasts, while the fifth chakra is located in the throat. The sixth chakra, also referred to as the third eye, is located between the [eye] brows, and the seventh, or crown chakra, which faces upward, is located at the top of the head. (Bruyere 1989, 67)

Each chakra energy possesses gifts. We all have all these gifts, but the enneagram might suggest that, though we can learn to become conscious of and open to all of them, we lack integration of one, and that particular under-functioning energy leaves us prey to compulsions. Now we look at how that lack of integration may play out.

The First Chakra, also called the Root Chakra, is the seat of health and well being, and a strong concern to keep them secure. "Change is generally experienced as threatening, and fear of death tends to be repressed. Causality is attributed to external circumstances rather than oneself, and unacceptable impulses are projected onto others." (Vaughan, 101) "The Self, asleep at this level, seems to be the victim of unconscious impulses and outside circumstances." "The strength and inertia of this worldview is represented by the image of an elephant. It is difficult to dislodge and sometimes runs amok." (102)

Strength, inertia, unconscious impulses, a not fully conscious attention, projection, and change as threatening, are all familiar to enneagram readers as observable traits of the compulsed #9, people who experience a dearth of energy. Chakra insights would tell us that these people are, quite literally, sitting on their desired energy and its concomitant well-being. For #9s who practice chakra discipline, an open and vital first chakra assists mightily their overall wellness and the balance of positive energies for living as well as for attentive prayer. Such qualities as grounding, peace, openness, an uncluttered view, and patience seem promised results.

The Second Chakra, called the Navel Chakra, is also called the hara, the point where powerful energies centrally emanate: emotional, erotic, life-zest, religious, creative, co-creative. "This chakra is associated with sexuality or general life-expansiveness." (103) It has the energy of a can-do gusto.

When #8s live out the negative energies of this chakra, such as overindulgence in food, sex, self-importance, passion, or desire to possess, they are caught in a trap of purposelessness and impotence. But these people can be very giving and caring, even passionate in their caring or love, they can be tolerant of others and ideas, and produce creatively through gifted intuition. Their good health and strength are often a reassurance to others. Opening this chakra could mean for the #8 a release from negative power-sensitive issues, an invitation to work harmoniously with God and others, and the gift of gathering one's whole being into this open chakra in surrender to God. Here is, perhaps, the essence of gut-centered prayer.

The Third Chakra, also called the Solar Plexus Chakra, is the seat of the hot emotions, such as anger, the fight-or-flight syndrome, and strong will and intentionality. Here is "an underlying desire for control in order to have things be the way one wants them to be. At this level, a person is likely to have strong opinions and an egocentric investment in being right. Conflicts arise when others do not agree with a particular point of view, as one feels threatened by differing perspectives and dissenting opinions." (105) There is a tendency to take in more than can be assimilated in a healthy way, to insist on what might be useful to make a thing better, whether it is needed or not.

For the #1 to open this chakra is to invite the release of that will to control, it is to let go, to balance out to an inner self-control, a more peaceful mastery of desire. From this letting go can flow more quiet energy, along with an awakening to being transformed without the feeling of having to do it all oneself, or that pulling oneself up by the bootstraps to which #1s are prone. These people can then experience an inner silent radiance that enables them to hand all over to God, to come then to a stillness that is their chief good.

The Fourth Chakra, the Heart Chakra, moves from the hot emotions to the subtler ones, such as compassion, love, and expansiveness. Energies locked into this center would show negatively as an emotional imbalance that represses a healthy love of self and expresses a pseudo compassion for others. But to open this chakra, to restore its real balance ". . . One must have given up the desire to be noticed or to be the center of attention" (108), or, to put it in terms of the #2 compulsion, to do for others always with the hook of approval. When the chakra is opened in a healthy integration "The oneness of all beings is intuited, and values shift accordingly in the direction of compassion, cooperation, and selfless service." (108)

A humble knowing of one's own lovableness, as well as one's needs, can encourage the #2 to allow this chakra its native expansiveness, peaceful acceptance, and balanced understanding. Divine and unconditional love, experienced here as a deeply inner Other, can teach the warm and giving love that expands into others' lives, and invests the pray-er with kindness, forgiveness, and a genuine being-for-others. "Love is no longer sought for personal gratification, but is offered out of gratitude for the fullness of an inner source." (108)

The Fifth or Throat Chakra. As the fourth chakra moves us out of the realm of the physical and into that of the Other, the fifth opens us to ". . . a spiritual orientation in ordinary life." (110) "Becoming aware of the creative power of consciousness associated with the fifth chakra means taking responsibility for thought as well as behavior." (111) Here is the energy of communication, which, if it is blocked in the compulsed #4, leads to the misunderstanding #4s dread, or to problems with speech, or to expressions stuck in the throat, to incomplete discernment or unwise words, and to the negative inwardness of depression. The opening of this chakra connects throat and ears. "Training at this level means learning to listen internally to oneself and externally to others. In order to listen, one must learn to be quiet. Both speech and internal chatter must therefore be controlled" (110)

With this chakra opened, the #4 can offer creative expression in speech, writing, and the arts, be trusted, wise, gentle, and kind, and possess integration of body, mind, and spirit, as the placement of this chakra suggests. And there is a sense of the Self. "The all-encompassing Self is perceived as ultimate reality. Concepts and thoughts are seen to have substantive reality and far-reaching effects. But concept is powerful here as an expression of experience, not as an abstract intellectual construct." (110) And if the #4 is one who has the experience of hearing "more distinctly the subtle messages of the Self, whether audible or inaudible." (111), (s)he will be listening where God speaks within in quiet truth.

The Sixth Chakra, mid-forehead, between and above the eyebrows, is the powerful chakra often called the third eye, "the realm of ideal perception." (111) This would, fittingly, be the home-energy of the enneagram #5, who would suffer, if the chakra is blocked, from tensions and headaches, even eye problems, a lack of concentration and clarity, a fear of not knowing, and, in consequence, a cynical attitude. All these cause the person to withdraw from the real world, to live detached from it. But the healthy energy of this chakra is full of gifts. "Mind at this level is more subtle; more spiritual gifts are bestowed as it awakens. Fears are dispelled by personal experience." (112)

The enlightened #5 discovers soul and peace of mind. The gift of insight is given abundantly, and the deeper gift of wisdom, an ideal for the #5, comes to flower, particularly as meditation moves the understanding beyond duality. "In the sixth chakra, the God that was dormant in the lower chakras is fully awake. This center is the place of union with the deity, where one knows the Self as psyche." (111)

"In meditation at this level all colors, lights, and images disappear and the mind rests in the white light of the void." (112) Or, in Christian prayer, in the light of God, beyond where sight can go.

The Seventh, or Crown Chakra. This chakra energy is full of inspiration, idealism, perceptions that transcend space and time, and a sense of the path of other chakra energies leading to this fullness. A sense of the plan, as it were, of human energies is much in harmony with the enneatype #7, the planner who likes cosmic spaces and endless options, who likes to view from above all interconnections and possibilities, in the excitement of heightened consciousness. But a #7 in whom this chakra is closed, whose capacities are confined and restless, will suffer a disturbing "monkey mind," with its attendant confusion. Lack of discipline and inspiration, fearfulness, hesitancy, and a loss of stability may follow, along with the stimulus of hyperactivity or its reverse, depression.

The open crown chakra is open also to the infinite, to the wisdom of the divine, and to a fully spiritual will. The invitation here is to union of the human personality with the higher Self, and beyond that, to a oneness with the divine. The enneagram #7 who is grounded in the human, the Self, and God, will indeed reach through this integration to the Source of all light.

The Chakra Experience is one that includes all seven energy centers. You may notice as you open your chakras that the one of your own enneagram type is hardest to open, perhaps because you are not aware of the unconscious avoidances or defenses stored there, or the fixation or passion. That chakra may offer a psychological and physical release to balance negative compulsions when you become conscious of its blockage, and open it to its positive energies. You might also open the positive arrow energy of your type; e.g., as a #4, I spend time with the solar plexus chakra to invite balance from #1 energy, as well as the heart chakra, inviting positive #2 arrow input.

But what does it mean to open a chakra? It means collecting your attention and focusing it on the particular energy center, gathering all your awareness there, breathing from it, and letting it expand and activate. What you put your attention to is activated. As the saying is: "Where attention goes, energy flows," whether for good or for ill. Mantras or visualization may prove helpful for focusing attention.

But of particular interest here are the prayer possibilities, as needed, from each or any chakra: first chakra, a grounding and settledness; second, surrender of the whole being; third, release of control issues; fourth, openness to divine love; fifth, contemplative communion; sixth, a mind open to God's wisdom; and seventh, a oneness with the Infinite. We have within us a wealth of gifts!

You will notice, as happens in patterns of seven, that the shock points of the enneagram, the #3 and #6, do not have their equivalents among the major chakras. Perhaps they would find a compatible combination in two or more of the centers, but in any case, all of us can access and use all of the chakras for our benefit. And I hope these comments have benefited those of you who do use this powerful system of energy centers, and who want to incorporate them into your enneagram style.

References

Assagioli, Roberto. 1965. *Psychosynthesis, A Collection of Basic Writings*. New York: Penguin Books.

Augustine, 1960. *The Confessions of St. Augustine*. Translated by John K. Ryan. Garden City: Image Books.

Bruyere, Rosalyn L. and Jeanne Farrens. 1989. *Wheels of Light*. Vol. 1. Arcadia: Bonn Productions.

The Cloud of Unknowing. 1973. Edited by William Johnston. Garden City: Image Books.

Gendlin, Eugene. 1982. *Focusing*. New York: Bantam Books.

A Letter of Private Direction. 1965. Rendered by James Walsh. Springfield: Templegate Publishers.

Merton, Thomas. 1948. *A Thomas Merton Reader*. New York: Harcourt, Brace & World, Inc.

Naranjo, Claudio. 1990. *Ennea-Type Structures*. Nevada City: Gateways/IDHHB, Inc.

_____. 1990. *How To Be*. Los Angeles: Jeremy P. Tarcher, Inc.

Teilhard de Chardin, Pierre. 1961. *Hymn of the Universe*. Translated by Gerald Vann. New York: Harper & Row.

_____. 1976. *The Heart of Matter*. Translated by Rene Hague. New York: Harcourt Brace Jovanovich.

Teresa of Avila. 1976. *The Collected Works of St. Teresa of Avila*. Vol. 1. Translated by Kieran Kavanaugh and Otilio Rodriguez. Washington, DC: ICS Publications.

_____. 1980. *The Collected Works of St. Teresa of Avila*. Vol. 2. Translated by Kieran Kavanaugh and Otilio Rodriguez. Washington, DC: ICS Publications.

Therese of Lisieux. 1958. *Autobiography of St. Therese of Lisieux*. Translated by Ronald Knox. New York: P. J. Kenedy & Sons.

Tobin, Mary Luke. 1983. Merton on Prayer: Start Where You Are. *Praying*. No. 1. October, 11–16.

Vaughan, Frances. 1995. *The Inward Arc. Healing in Psychotherapy and Spirituality.* Nevada City: Blue Dolphin Publishing.

Wagner, Jerome P. 1980. The Enneagram System of Personality Typology. diss. Loyola University, Chicago.

Zuercher, Suzanne. 1992. *Enneagram Spirituality.* Notre Dame, IN: Ave Maria Press.

_____. 1993. *Enneagram Companions.* Notre Dame, IN: Ave Maria Press.

Some other Resources for Basic Enneagram Studies

Baron, Renee, and Elizabeth Wagels. 1994. *The Enneagram Made Easy.* San Francisco: Harper.

_____. 1995. *Are You My Type, Am I Yours?* San Francisco: Harper.

Beesing, Maria, Robert J. Nogosek, and Patrick H. O'Leary. 1984. *The Enneagram, A Journey of Self Discovery.* Denville, NJ: Dimension Books, Inc.

Carmody, Leie, and Cathy Conheim. 1981. *So Who's a 10 In A World of 1 to 9?* San Diego: Ventures International.

Henry, Kathleen M. 1987. *The Book of Enneagram Prayers.* Jamaica Plain: Alabastar Jar Liturgical Arts.

Metz, Barbara, and John Burchill. 1987. *The Enneagram and Prayer.* Denvill, NJ: Dimension Books.

Naranjo, Claudio. 1994. *Character and Neurosis.* Nevada City: Gateways/IDHHB.

_____. 1997. *Transformation Through Insight.* Prescott: Hohm.

Palmer, Helen. 1988. *The Enneagram. Understanding Yourself and the Others in Your Life.* San Francisco: HarperCollins.

Riso, Don Richard. 1987. *Personality Types. Using the Enneagram for Self-Discovery.* Boston: Houghton Mifflin Company.

_____. 1990. *Understanding the Enneagram.* Boston: Houghton Mifflin Company.

_____. 1993. *Enneagram Transformations.* Boston: Houghton Mifflin Company.

Rohr, Richard, and Andreas Ebert. 1990. *Discovering the Enneagram.* New York: Crossroads Publishing Company.

Wagner, Jerome P. *Two Windows On The Self. The Enneagram and the Myers-Briggs.* Credence Cassettes SPCN 7900780823. Audiocassettes.

There are many other good basic resources, and many good authors not mentioned here in this short list. These are a few suggested starters, with an encouragement to launch out on what you might be drawn to.

About the Author

Rosaleen O'Sullivan is a native of San Francisco and a member of the Sisters of Mercy, Burlingame, California. She has an M.A. in Latin, along with theology, Jungian studies, and counseling, and is now a spiritual director and enneagram presenter. After twenty years in secondary education, followed by parish ministries and programs for working young adults, she graduated from the Institute for Spiritual Leadership in Chicago in 1982. Since then, she has been a frequent presenter of enneagram workshops and seminars, retreats, and study days for spiritual directors using the enneagram. After her basic workshop series, Rosaleen offers a day on prayer and the enneagram to help people with their own inner work and prayer styles. It was this day and the number of participants who found it enlightening for growth in inner awareness and simple modes of contemplative prayer, reflection, or just holy being, that led to this book.